# A FISTFUL OF MURDER

HAMILCAR NOIR | TRUE CRIME LIBRARY #5

Don Stradley

# a FISTFUL of MURDER

## The Fights and Crimes of Carlos Monzon

HAMILCAR NOIR

HARD-HITTING TRUE CRIME

ISBN: 978-1949590-31-9

Publisher's Cataloging-in-Publication Data
Names: Stradley, Don, author.
Title: Fistful of murder : the fights and crimes of Carlos Monzon / Don Stradley. Series: Hamilcar Noir. Description: Boston, MA: Hamilcar Publications, 2020.
Identifiers: LCCN: 2020937647 | ISBN 9781949590319
Subjects: LCSH Monzón, Carlos, 1942- | Boxers (Sports)—Argentina—Biography. | Marital violence—Argentina. | Women, Crimes against—Argentina. | Murder—Argentina—Mar del Plata. | BISAC BIOGRAPHY & AUTOBIOGRAPHY / Sports | SPORTS & RECREATION / Boxing | BIOGRAPHY & AUTOBIOGRAPHY / Cultural, Ethnic & Regional / Hispanic & Latino | TRUE CRIME / Murder / General
Classification: LCC GV1132.M67 .S77 2020 | DDC 796.8/3/092—dc23

Hamilcar Publications
*An imprint of* Hannibal Boxing Media
Ten Post Office Square, 8th Floor South
Boston, MA 02109
www.hamilcarpubs.com

*Printed in the United States of America*

*On the cover: Carlos Monzon and Alicia Muniz at a discotheque in Deauville, France, in 1983.* Getty Images

*Frontispiece: Monzon looks over the balcony at 1567 Pedro Zanni Street as police reconstruct the death of Alicia.* El Grafico/Getty Images

*For two men who inspired me with their writing and their friendship . . .*

*Bert Sugar (1936–2012)*

*Jack Olsen (1925–2002)*

*In the ring I understand everything.*
*It is outside where things get complicated.*

—Carlos Monzon

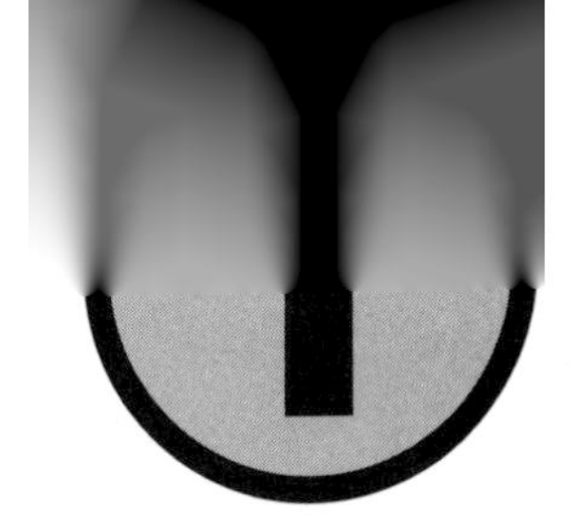

# The Void

She lay on the bricks, splattered like a grapefruit.

The woman was nearly nude, save for her flimsy white panties. In the dawn light, one could almost make out the spreading pool of blood under her head. She was thirty-two. Her name was Alicia Muniz.

The body was in the La Florida neighborhood of Mar del Plata, a resort city south of Buenos Aires, Argentina. At one time a popular seaside attraction, Mar del Plata was on a decline thanks to a growing drug presence. Despite the downturn, Argentine entertainers still rented homes there while they performed in neighboring theaters and cabarets. The address where Alicia Muniz's corpse was found, 1567 Pedro Zanni Street, was a house rented by Adrian Martel, a middle-aged actor who was appearing in a local stage production. Known as "El Facha" ("The Face"), Martel was a cocaine user who enjoyed providing his friends with drugs. He is also said to have hosted orgies, videotaping his show business pals as they indulged in sleazy activities. Alicia's estranged husband, Carlos Monzon, was staying with Martel for the season.

It was early Sunday, February 14, 1988. Martel's neighbors would say they'd heard angry voices at approximately 5:45 a.m. This wasn't unusual. Martel was the neighborhood cocaine connection; people were in and out of his place all the time. But this particular weekend was supposed to be about romance. Monzon would later explain that Alicia had come to Mar del Plata to reconcile after a separation. Their marriage was a wreck. He wanted a new start. Instead, something happened on the balcony. Alicia took a fifteen-foot drop and became a tabloid cover girl.

Details came out slowly. Monzon was no help. Nothing he said made sense.

Monzon was one of Argentina's most celebrated figures. A former boxing champion of legendary status, he had also acted in movies and enjoyed highly publicized affairs with beautiful actresses. He mingled with the wealthiest of the French Riviera and the elite of international cinema. Yet he'd spent most of the recent Argentine summer in seedy Mar del Plata. Like the failing city, Monzon rested on his faded glamour.

Monzon and Alicia had met a decade earlier. By outward appearances they were an ideal South American celebrity couple. She was a Uruguayan-born dancer, model, and actress. He was the aging superstar, an Argentine emblem. They looked stunning together. She was delicate, with light hair and fair skin. Her slightly upturned nose gave her a pixie look. He was tall with rugged features, a flowing mane of black hair. In photographs, Alicia gazed at him adoringly. Still, the relationship had been difficult from the start. "She is too young," Monzon once said of their thirteen-year age difference. "She doesn't know how to be with a famous person."

In his more reflective moods, Monzon would say that he wanted to buy a new home where he, Alicia, and their six-year-old son, Maximiliano, could live happily. But Monzon often terrorized Alicia with his temper. She had gone to the police on two occasions to file complaints against him.

In recent months, Alicia and little Maxi lived with her parents while she sought modeling work. She'd agreed to let Maxi spend some time with his father but had since heard that Facha Martel's house was a cocaine and sex hangout, not a safe place for a young boy. Also, Monzon owed Alicia money for Maxi's care. Though Monzon would insist Alicia had come to Mar del Plata for a weekend rendezvous, Alicia's friends and family would insist she was only there to visit Maxi, and to remove him from the unsavory surroundings. Alicia had told friends that she still loved Monzon, but couldn't go back to living with him.

Monzon was in the dusk of his celebrity. When he'd met Alicia, he was only one year removed from being the world's middleweight champion. Now he was forty-five and had reached that inevitable twilight faced by many ex-jocks: He was still famous, but no longer important. He had recently agreed to promote a line of sportswear bearing his name, and had just returned from France, where he'd appeared on a television show honoring great boxing champions. But these were minor dealings; most of the time he was drunk, wasting his evenings at nearby casinos, or harassing Alicia by phone. Sometimes he'd find out where she was staying. He'd show up in the middle of the night, well-oiled and making threats.

He had a history of domestic violence. The actress and talk-show host Susana Gimenez was romantically involved with Monzon for four years. She knew all about his unexpected rages. "He was very jealous and I couldn't even say hello to anyone," she said in 2014. Monzon admitted he had problems with anger. In a 1979 interview, he explained that violence "is my worst problem. All my friends tell me that when I get angry I should count to ten. But when I get to two, I explode." Friends of Alicia said she sometimes arrived for modeling jobs with bruised arms.

On the morning of February 14, the caretaker at the house, Carlos Guazzano, heard someone pounding on his door. Monzon was shouting.

There'd been an accident on the balcony. Alicia had fallen. Monzon had fallen, too.

An ambulance arrived. Monzon was taken to a hospital, where he was treated for injured ribs and a broken clavicle. Alicia's body was left behind in a twisted heap. According to reports given at the time, Monzon said nothing about Alicia during the ambulance ride. It wasn't until he was in the hospital that he made any sort of statement. He explained that Alicia had tumbled from the balcony into the void. Monzon remembered nothing else, only that there had been an argument, and that he woke up next to his wife's dead body.

The police didn't buy Monzon's weird story. He was arrested and charged with killing Alicia. In an oral testimony, Monzon told Judge Jorge Garcia Collins that he may have hit Alicia, but added, "I have hit women on other occasions, and nothing happened to any of them." He finished by saying, "I hit all of my women except one. My mother."

Argentine newspapers quickly filled their front pages with photos of Alicia's corpse. The image would eventually be everywhere, from glossy publications to cheap newsstand tabloids. As Americans would one day be overwhelmed by images of Nicole Brown Simpson and JonBenét Ramsey, so it was in Argentina with the nearly naked and bloody Alicia Muniz, facedown forever. Even an autopsy photo—an extreme closeup of Alicia's shattered head and blackened right eye—would turn up in newspaper and magazine layouts, anything to magnify the horror of her death. "The photo seemed to speak," said Argentine journalist Jorge Joury, "as if asking us to investigate thoroughly and get to the truth."

Two days later, with his torso swathed in bandages, Monzon returned to the crime scene with investigators. He stood on the balcony, trying to re-create the incident of Sunday morning. As Monzon spoke, onlookers heckled him from the street. An estimated five hundred people had come to see the humiliated ex-boxer. A chant began: "Murderer! Murderer!" A second chant went up in response: "Champion! Champion!" On it went for several minutes—"Champion!" "Murderer!" "Champion!" "Murderer!" The noise drew more onlookers, until the lawns of nearby neighbors were entirely trampled by spectators. The chanting grew louder, even when mounted police arrived to disperse the crowd.

Monzon told a confusing and conflicting story. The argument was about money, he said.

He remembered fighting with Alicia, but not how she'd fallen over the railing. His best guess was that she had slipped and that he fell trying to save her. He'd been drunk, after all.

Argentina was in the middle of ongoing political turmoil and a teetering economy, but the Monzon case dominated the news. Coverage was spiced with lurid tales from Monzon's past, including his many arrests for assault. According to Alicia's mother, Monzon had threatened to kill Alicia more than once.

Then, two days after Monzon offered his vague description of events, the medical examiners reported a discovery: Alicia had been strangled. This detail inspired the theory that Monzon had throttled Alicia into unconsciousness before dumping her off the balcony.

On February 19, 1988, Judge Guillermo Vallejos ordered Monzon to be transferred to a federal prison in nearby Batán. Monzon was charged under Argentine law with non-aggravated murder, meaning murder without premeditation. If found guilty, he faced a maximum of twenty-five years in prison.

Exactly one month later, Muniz family lawyer Rodolfo Vega Lecich announced that new medical evidence revealed that Alicia was dead before she went over the balcony. The charges against Monzon were quickly changed to aggravated murder, and possibly a life sentence.

By this time, as Monzon was undergoing psychiatric testing, journalists were debating the causes of Alicia's death. Was it Argentina's macho society gone haywire, or was it because Alicia had perhaps been unfaithful? Was Monzon to be blamed for his bad temper or the effects of alcohol? He was just an ignorant boxer, after all. Or was the entire event, as Monzon insisted, an accident?

The case shook Argentina. But no matter how many gaudy headlines appeared, none could say as much as the mob on Pedro Zanni Street, their words endlessly spinning like two sides of a coin flipped into the abyss: Champion . . . murderer . . . champion . . .

Murderer.

◆ ◆ ◆

The death of Alicia Muniz wasn't a complete surprise to anyone who knew Carlos Monzon. The surprise was that no one else had died in his company.

He had a volcanic temper. He drank heavily and used cocaine. He drove recklessly, had a fascination with guns, and had been arrested many times for physical assaults. In February of 1988, with his personal life in shreds, Monzon had finally reached the nadir of an existence defined by hostility, with nothing to obstruct his most savage instincts.

If they'd indeed been fighting about money—and we only have Monzon's word on that—he wasn't about to let Alicia get her way. And, in a gesture that would haunt him for the rest of his life, telling a judge that he'd routinely hit women reflected both his mental makeup and the macho male culture of Argentina. Monzon craved control. He also understood his place in the pantheon of Argentine athletes, a lofty position that had provided a kind of protective blanket for even his most vicious behavior.

But as sickening as the killing of Alicia Muniz was, the story of Carlos Monzon is more than a murder story. It is also the tale of a once-great fighter who dominated his field at a time when boxing flourished in South America. It was a time when the prince of Monaco always had a good seat at the fights, and the French Riviera was where big-money bouts were born and brokered. It was when Italian boxing promoters dabbled in producing films, boxers acted in movies, and wealthy French actors became fight promoters. Most boxing fans recall the 1970s as the Muhammad

Ali era, but in Argentina and parts of Europe, it was the decade of Monzon.

Monzon had been a rarity in boxing in that he was truly a champion with an international following. During a title reign that spanned from 1970 to 1977, his revolving base of operation included Buenos Aires, Rome, Paris, and Monte Carlo. In Buenos Aires he entered the ring smiling and blowing kisses. Yet Monzon didn't love Buenos Aires; it was too loud for him. Declaring that he preferred rural life made him even more beloved in Argentina's backwaters. Sure, he mingled with movie stars and wore tailored clothes, but he was still seen as a simple Argentine of indigenous blood. This image of Monzon as an earthy man of the people, no doubt, is one of the reasons he was idolized even after his conviction for a hideous crime.

The importance of Monzon to Argentina had much to do with the country's political climate of the era. After a military overthrow of the government in 1966, the country was enduring a time of assassinations, repression, and state-sponsored terrorism. For Argentines, Monzon represented the spirit of the gaucho, the cowboy, self-reliant with a hint of the unruly. Defiance in the face of oppression is always appealing.

Rome was different. The Italians saw Monzon as the thug who had annihilated their beloved champion, Nino Benvenuti. Sometimes the Italian crowds jeered Monzon and pelted him with garbage. The gambling crowd in Monaco embraced Monzon, but they viewed him as a bit of a bumpkin, a feral street kid who owned some expensive suits but couldn't hide his dirty neck. By the end of his championship reign, as he traveled with a sexy girlfriend on his arm and a caravan of luggage, Monzon was, indeed, a top-line Monte Carlo attraction, a jet-set Neanderthal who had finally learned to eat with a knife and fork.

Monzon acquired a mystique in Paris that was almost otherworldly. Intrigued by his stone expression, Parisian newspapers made a game of creating new nicknames for Monzon, including "The Prince of Air and Darkness" and "The Cold Monster." Welsh writer Clive Gammon once commented that the French regarded Monzon not as an athlete, but as "some terrible supernatural force hidden behind unexpressive Amerindian features."

The French were on to something. Over time there were hints of a darker self that existed within Monzon's image, and comments that, in hindsight, are spooky. Rodolfo Sabbatini, the Italian promoter behind several of Monzon's bouts, once sent his personal bodyguard to work for Monzon while the champion was in training. Sabbatini was asked if this was to protect Monzon from the public.

No, he said. It was the public that needed protection from Monzon.

# Rome, 11/7/1970

Monzon won the middleweight championship with a right hand to the jaw. It landed with such impact that one could almost see the word **POW** light up over Nino Benvenuti's head. It was November 1970, two and a half years into Benvenuti's second reign as champion; the Italian audience at Rome's Palazzetto dello Sport watched in disbelief as their hero collapsed to his knees, his forehead touching the canvas.

It was inconceivable that Benvenuti would lose in Rome. He'd fought there more than thirty times and had never lost. Against Monzon, who rarely fought outside of Argentina, Benvenuti was a three-to-one favorite. Yet Italy's champion was down. He tried to rise but was so disoriented that German referee Rudolph Durst waved the fight over. Monzon's punch had been just about perfect, a right hand straight from the slaughterhouse. As Monzon had said before the bout, he hadn't come to Rome "just for sightseeing." Then again, prior to the fight Monzon had done the most touristy of things: He stopped by the famous Trevi Fountain and tossed a coin into it, supposedly guaranteeing him a return to Rome. He'd also visited the Vatican and prayed for a victory.

Monzon had spent the days before the bout playing psychological games with Benvenuti. He acted bored during interviews. During a press lunch he raised his fork and yelled, "This is what I'll do to Nino!" Then he violently stabbed the hunk of broiled chicken on his plate. Monzon's aura of serene and sober confidence left Benvenuti exasperated. Monzon's mind games continued right up until moments before the fight. With his and Benvenuti's dressing rooms separated by only a thin wall, Monzon asked Luna Park's hefty publicist Alfredo Capece to pound on the walls with his meaty fists. "The noise," Monzon later recalled, "was barbaric." Monzon couldn't have risked hitting the walls himself, since his hands had always been delicate, but Capece was free to punch away—Boom! Boom! Boom!—until some Italian journalists asked what was going on. They were told, "It's just Monzon warming up." Word, of course, reached Benvenuti.

Monzon also did a good psych job on himself. In perhaps the most revealing comment he ever made about his boxing mindset, he wrote in his memoir *My True Life*, "In the previous days I got into my head that Benvenuti was a son of a bitch who did not deserve to live, who had to be killed in the ring. If he won, I died and it was my last chance."

Benvenuti doomed himself at the weigh-in when he playfully tweaked Monzon's ass. Monzon could tease a rival, but to be mocked was unbearable. As Monzon said in *My True Life*, "I wanted to tear his head off."

The fight was ugly, both men skirting the thin line between boxing and street fighting. The Italian fans were astonished by Monzon's treatment of Benvenuti. If Benvenuti boxed from the outside, Monzon would ram him with jabs and straight rights. If Benvenuti tried to move inside, Monzon responded with head butts, elbows, and chops to the neck. If Benvenuti fouled, Monzon would foul him twice in return. If Benvenuti tried to rest during the clinches, Monzon would jam his shoulder into his mouth. In the seventh, Monzon stunned Benvenuti and nearly knocked him down. During the tenth the crowd chanted "Nino! Nino!" but the tired champion's punches were futile.

Benvenuti wasn't a great fighter, but he was a very good one. Along with two terms as middleweight champion, he'd won a gold medal at the 1960 Rome Olympics. He was a refined athlete who appreciated literature and classical music; he trained at a gym decorated with Renoir reproductions and a carpeted marble staircase. He'd already appeared in a film, a mediocre spaghetti western called *Alive or Preferably Dead*. There was a sense that, at thirty-two, Benvenuti was ready to leave boxing and go into the movie business or politics. Still, his devoted followers were certain he had enough left to beat this uncouth challenger.

Even in Argentina, there were doubts about Monzon.

"Monzon was something special," recalled former sports editor of *La Nacion* Carlos Losauro in a 2010 interview, "because he smoked a lot and had many vices. But thirty days before each fight, the guy cut everything, locked himself in the gym and prepared himself. However, almost nobody expected him to win. He went to Italy to lose."

At a fraction under six feet tall, weighing just under 160 pounds, with a 76.5-inch reach that remains one of the longest in middleweight history, Monzon looked gangly as a scarecrow. Yet with each passing round, he appeared to grow bigger and more powerful. The Italians booed him, at one point bombarding the ring with orange peels and half-eaten sandwiches. Monzon seemed to inhale the bedlam and draw strength from it.

The bout ended at 1:57 of the twelfth round. Benvenuti's outraged supporters tried to storm the ring and attack the referee, only to be beaten back by police. In the tumult, Monzon's handlers lifted the new champion to their shoulders; a dazed and battered Benvenuti was helped onto his stool where he sat for several minutes, barely comprehending the hell that had been dropped on him.

"Benvenuti had the glamour," Monzon said. "His picture was everywhere. But I knew from the minute we signed the contract I would beat him."

It was a matter of timing, as is the case with most boxing successes. Benvenuti was at the end of his career, while Monzon's confidence was at its peak. Of course, Monzon's confidence was always a thing of legend—he once said, "the pope was the only man before whom I felt small,"—but Monzon's self-assurance hadn't come easily. It hadn't come from Argentine boxing fans, who had previously treated him with something like indifference, and it hadn't come from the Italian press, who had called him many dreadful names prior to the bout. And it hadn't come from his family environment or his childhood, which he'd barely survived.

Monzon's confidence was his own creation. He knitted it from childish ideas about power and control, and he wore it like a bulletproof vest. The Monzon that was unleashed on the boxing world—a brutal, arrogant, remorseless, man—was actually the handiwork of a sick little boy with weak bones, a boy who despised his poor surroundings and dreamed of being a Wild West gunman.

◆ ◆ ◆

Carlos Monzon was born in the La Flecha neighborhood of San Javier, a small, northeastern city in the province of Santa Fe, on August 7, 1942. One of twelve children born to Roque and Amalia Ladesma Monzon, he was allegedly the biggest baby ever seen in San Javier. He was born in his family's shack on Alvear Street, on a blanket spread out on a dirt floor. Fittingly, a violent rainstorm raged outside.

Much about Monzon's early years is hazy. It's been customary to list his middle name as Roque, after his father, but official documents list him as simply "Carlos Monzon," with no middle name. Even the exact order of Monzon's siblings has been in dispute, with early sources listing him as the seventh child of Roque and Amalia, though researchers uncovered another Monzon child, making Carlos the eighth. Monzon's alleged Indian background has also been debated, with many researchers dismissing old publicity hype about his "Indian warrior blood." Though San Javier elders insist the Monzons were indigenous, many argue that Monzon was more likely a mestizo, a mix of European and Latin American races.

Monzon's home was a small straw hovel with a thatched roof, with rooms separated by tarps. Like their neighbors, they lived a meager existence in a house that one friend recalled as more "like a nest." There was a persistent fear of flooding from the San Javier River and of the diseases that thrived in the constant dampness. Sometimes the Monzons had to hunt for food. A typical day for young Carlos saw him rising early with his brothers to hunt swamp rodents, including capybaras weighing more than one hundred pounds. From there they'd spend a lazy afternoon by the river, making up games, killing snakes. When they had a few coins, Monzon and his friends went to the local movie theater. After the show, they'd ride their own horses in and out of town at full gallop, pretending to be American cowboys.

Monzon's favorite character in those days was the Durango Kid. Played by Charles Starrett throughout the 1940s for Columbia Pictures, the Kid was an avenging gunman known for the black kerchief he wore to protect his identity. The Kid stormed through nearly fifty films and inspired a line of Durango Kid comics. The colorful magazines left such an imprint on Monzon's imagination that he mentioned them in his first memoir, *My True Life*, recalling the fun he had imitating the masked man, riding his horse and waving an imaginary six-gun in the air. In a second memoir published only in France, Monzon described the mystery gunman as "my idol" and recalled how the comic books told of "miraculous adventures that dazzled me."

While young Carlos lost himself in fantasies of B-movie gunslingers, he remained under the heel of extreme poverty. By age six he was working as a shoeshine boy to help his family.

Monzon's upbringing was also marked by health problems and malnutrition. His family couldn't afford vaccinations, which left him vulnerable to illnesses, including a painful bout of childhood rickets. Underprivileged and sickly, Monzon sometimes felt people were laughing at him. Amilcar Brusa, the revered boxing trainer who would soon mentor him, would say Monzon was "always a bully in the ring, but in his life he was a defenseless boy."

Monzon was nine when his family moved to the provincial capital where some of his older siblings had found work. The Monzons settled in West Barranquitas, a downtrodden Santa Fe neighborhood. It was there that Monzon began noticing the difference between Argentina's indigenous people and the "gringos," the Swiss, Italian, German, and Polish, who always seemed to have money and owned the local businesses. For the nine-year-old Monzon, it was devastating to learn that not everyone was as poor as his family. Monzon later told a journalist that when he saw wealthy people drive by in shiny cars, he yearned to go with them and leave his family behind. These thoughts brought on feelings of guilt, but the urge to escape his environment was strong.

On the streets of Santa Fe, Monzon realized, "you had to always be prepared to fight, to defend what little you had." As a teen, Monzon's readiness to fight was soon getting him in trouble with the police. He never offered great detail but suggested the Santa Fe cops put him through some horrific treatment.

This most surely was the battlefield where Monzon was formed. He would grow up known for a cold glare that could've had many origins, perhaps a mistrust of the police, or because of a distant father who was too busy working to show anything like parental love. The most likely basis, however, was his being confronted every day with a vision of rock-bottom poverty. "In the city we lost our spirit," Monzon said. "We had always been poor. Now we were poor and bitter."

The effect of extreme deprivation on a child's development can include everything from high levels of chronic stress to a noticeable atrophy of the hippocampus, the part of the brain that regulates emotional responses and memory. Researchers have found that an upbringing such as Monzon's can have an impact identical to post-traumatic stress disorder. To a child, the wild uncertainties of severe poverty can have the same devastating effect of being abandoned or exposed to violence during war. Monzon's young life was chaotic, full of uncertainty. He didn't know if he'd have food or if he'd come down with another illness. He didn't know if a flood would wipe out his home, if some other boy would try to steal his shoeshine money, or if he would have another rough encounter with the police.

It is possible that Carlos Monzon learned at an early age to deal with his fears in the way many poor males did. What makes you feel bad, what torments you, no matter how overwhelming—simply lash out at it instead of letting yourself be backed into a corner.

It was probably in Santa Fe, then, that the cold glare was developed. In the decades to come, Monzon's wicked stare would become chillier and scarier. It would take time, though, until his physical power was enough to back up his intense expression, but the end result was a glare that would become his trademark: a cold, mean look that said FUCK OFF.

Monzon remained suspicious of people throughout his life. The stare never softened. New York sportswriter Michael Katz recalled that Monzon's eyes "were cold as ice. He said he didn't want to talk; you turned and walked away. You did not argue."

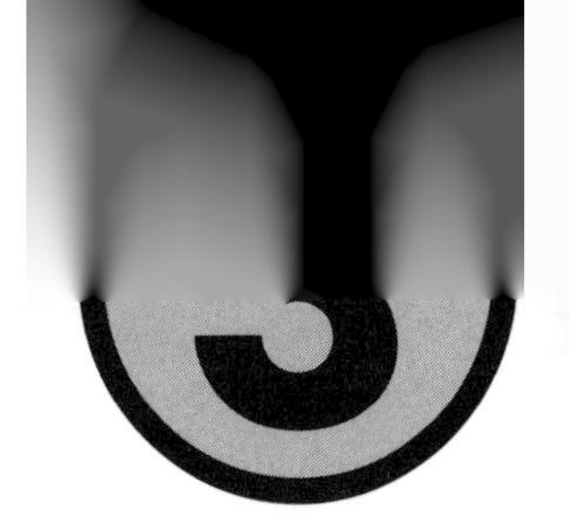

# "They Killed Themselves with Laughter"

Monzon first arrived at the Club Atlético Unión, Amilcar Brusa's Santa Fe gym, in 1960. He was seventeen at the time with the bony physique of an emaciated street dog. And he was ready to fight.

Monzon could never fully explain his attraction to boxing. He claimed he'd been intrigued by Luis "Gato" Aranda, a Santa Fe boxer who competed at the 1960 Olympics. He also said he'd been mesmerized by a newspaper photo of Argentine lightweight Jose Maria Gatica driving a flashy 1946 Mercury. Like Monzon, Gatica had been a shoeshine boy. "I saw myself reflected in him," Monzon said. "I began daydreaming that my name was in the newspapers, people were shouting 'Monzon!' and that I had so much money it was falling out of my pockets."

Monzon wasn't thinking about being rich like Gatica. He wanted, as he put it, "just enough to get out of the shit." His mother objected to him fighting, but Monzon had already been through many years of low-paying labor jobs and imagined boxing could be his way out of poverty. He didn't want to replay the lives of his parents with their dozen hungry children. He also needed money. He had recently impregnated a Santa Fe girl named Zulema Encarnación Torres and had a son, Carlos Alberto. If fighting was the way to riches, Monzon was game. "I cannot be so sadistic to say that I felt pleasure in fighting," Monzon said, "but I do say that I had no fear."

Monzon had some experience as an amateur boxer before he met Brusa, but he was awkward, unfinished. Brusa fed him, got him healthy. Brusa's gym was primitive, with dirt on the floor and mud in the basement, full of fighters so poor they couldn't afford shoes. Monzon fit in with the squalor. He also took a liking to Brusa, a tall, pear-shaped man with neatly combed hair and endless patience. "My fighters are my friends," Brusa liked to say. Brusa liked Monzon's mean, hungry look but could sense he was going to be difficult. Violence and hate seemed to emanate from the young man's bones. Monzon didn't particularly enjoy training, either. In the gym, Monzon said, a fighter might start to doubt himself. But entering the ring on fight night was like coming home. At that moment, Monzon said, "I feel mean, but good."

Still, Monzon wasn't living the Spartan lifestyle required for boxing success. He subsisted on pizza, cigarettes, and cheap wine. He was respectful in front of Brusa, but away from the gym, he did as he pleased. Monzon also had an entourage of unemployed young drifters who followed him everywhere, as if he were the neighborhood overlord. To Brusa's annoyance, Monzon's lackeys even accompanied him to the gym.

Brusa, meanwhile, took special care in developing Monzon, hiding his weaknesses and magnifying his strengths. Monzon wasn't particularly quick or graceful, so Brusa kept him stationary and made him into a veritable punching machine. Brusa taught all of his fighters how to throw the right hand with maximum impact. Monzon threw his right like a dagger, but downplayed Brusa's influence. "It is just how I hit naturally," Monzon said. Monzon liked when he could punch a sparring partner and not be struck in return. Boxing, he learned, wasn't merely an exercise in brute force; it was tactical. Monzon was nearly illiterate, with no more than two or three years of schooling, but he took pride in being smarter than his opponents. Brusa once said that Monzon may not have been stylish in the ring, "but his mind was at work all the time."

Still, early audiences laughed at Monzon, screaming out insults about his skinny body. "They killed themselves with laughter," Monzon said. Overcome with embarrassment, he'd forget everything Brusa had taught him about boxing. Instead, he'd leap at his opponent and throw wild punches. His anger only made him ineffective. A rival with a bit of experience could simply dance away from him as Monzon lumbered forward, drawing more laughs from the crowd. It took months before Monzon learned to stay calm in the ring. Once he did, he began ripping through the local amateur ranks, dominating opponents with his long reach and coiled power.

After posting a respectable amateur record of 73-6-8, Monzon made his professional debut on Wednesday, February 6, 1963. At a midsize soccer stadium in Rafaela, Santa Fe, in the only bout of the evening, Monzon stopped Ramon Montenegro in two rounds. He would go on to win seven of his first eight fights by knockout. Monzon's potent right hand would inspire journalist Julio Cantero to dub him "Escopeta" ("Shotgun").

But even as he improved in the ring, Monzon was uncontrollable on the streets. Brusa often received phone calls in the middle of the night to get his young tiger out of jail. The reformed street fighter had graduated to busting up saloons. Brusa, who also coached the police boxing team, would use his connections to set Monzon free. The joke around Brusa's gym was that Monzon would be paroled on Saturdays so he could fight, then he'd be back in the slammer by Sunday.

Brusa's quickness to cover for him may have helped nurture a narcissistic tendency in Monzon. Though still shockingly poor, Monzon had developed an exaggerated image of himself, a feeling that he was above the law. Going from undernourished child to a macho male powerhouse made him feel not only indestructible, but in charge of his fate. With his flunkies and Brusa nourishing his ego, this feeling of specialness was intoxicating. It was also delicate, and when his fantasy of himself was threatened, he could become moody. This was also apparent in the ring. "One thing I didn't like about him as a fighter," said Emile Griffith, was that "he seemed to get a little discouraged if he landed a good one and the other guy . . . didn't act hurt." Indeed, when Monzon was against an opponent who dared fight back, he seemed to lose interest. His scowl would turn into a pout and it could take several rounds for him to get back into the fight. This reaction to fighters who didn't cower from him likely cost him some bouts that he should've won in both his amateur and early pro career.

Monzon, meanwhile, was learning something beyond hooks and jabs. Boxing had brought him a type of eminence. Over time, Monzon didn't even need Brusa to bail him out. If the Santa Fe police picked him up for some transgression, he merely had to identify himself. He'd explain his case and be allowed to go home. Where he once feared the police, now he counted them as allies. Incidents that could've turned out much worse instead fed his growing arrogance. Santa Fe was his, and no saloon was safe.

And heaven help the idiot who dared laugh at Carlos Monzon.

◆ ◆ ◆

During this same era, psychiatry was breaking ground in the study of a pathology called "narcissistic personality disorder." Leading the charge was Heinz Kohut, an Austrian-American psychiatrist out of Chicago. While Monzon was destroying barrooms, Kohut and others built upon ideas put forth by Sigmund Freud, concluding that a narcissist could be identified by certain traits. Simply put, the narcissist wasn't merely self-absorbed. He was actually creating a grand image to compensate for massive insecurities. He knew the truth about himself, but made it his life's mission to keep anyone else from knowing. He was, in short, working behind a façade—a deceiver who presented an attractive exterior but, when the false front crumbled to reveal the frightened, damaged soul underneath, was likely to overreact with a sudden burst of anger, or "narcissistic rage."

Even with the traits of a narcissist, Monzon could've lived a less brutal life. Not all narcissists are violent or abusive to women. Monzon, however, was a toxic mix. The effect of his deprived background and his growing reliance on alcohol were a pair of dark demons, but just as substantial was the sustenance he found on the street and in the ring, where he was somebody.

An outsize sense of entitlement, a tenuous sense of self-worth, conflicted feelings about one's upbringing, extreme arrogance as well as a grandiose self-image, an ability to be charming, an insatiable appetite for praise and admiration, the need for total control, extreme jealousy, and eruptions of anger would all be noted as signs of narcissism. Sam Vaknin, author of *Malignant Self-Love: Narcissism Revisited*, described perhaps the most troubling aspect of the narcissist: They demand to be recognized for their uniqueness, while never appreciating anyone else. "The narcissist devours people," he said, "consumes their output, and casts the empty, writhing shells aside."

Add them up, and the traits describe Carlos Monzon.

◆ ◆ ◆

In 1962, nineteen-year-old Monzon married fifteen-year-old Mercedes Beatriz Garcia. They lived in her family's two-room shack, sharing a mattress on the floor.

Brusa advised Monzon to buy a small piece of land and build his own place. With help from his father, Monzon built a house made of mud with a thatched roof. For Mercedes, who came from an even poorer family than Monzon and had already endured her share of tragedies, it was livable. In a short time they had two children, Sylvia Beatriz and Abel Ricardo. As Monzon made more money, he added more rooms to their little mud house. Used often in his early publicity was a photograph of Monzon from this period, pushing a wheelbarrow and looking like a happy man of the soil.

Being a family man didn't curb Monzon's antisocial ways. During this part of his career, he was arrested for starting a riot at a soccer game and brawling on a public bus. According to some sources he even tried his hand at pimping. An early police report cited arrests for "drunkenness, street quarrels, and contempt." When the Santa Fe police suggested Monzon leave town for a while, Brusa booked a series of fights for him in Brazil.

By October of 1964, Monzon had compiled an unspectacular pro record of 16-3, with one no-contest. In time there also were a high number of draws on Monzon's ledger. To Monzon's credit, he avenged all of his losses and most of his draws. The exception was a June 1966 draw with Ubaldo Marcos Bustos in Rio Gallegos. There was no rematch. Bustos retired from boxing with the distinction of being the only opponent Monzon never defeated. Though he finished with a record of 1-8-1, Bustos could always boast that he drew with Monzon, one of the great middleweights. Then again, during that period Monzon didn't appear destined for greatness.

Why didn't Monzon beat such a hapless character as Bustos? The truth could be that Monzon was simply erratic in those early years. Along with Griffith's point that Monzon grew dispirited if challenged, there was Monzon's own admission that he was often distracted by one thing or another, whether it was a sore hand, a recent arrest, or the fact that he had to get up early the next morning to go to one of his labor jobs. That this unfocused, difficult young man would later achieve so much in boxing was proof of his determination. For all of his bad behavior, Monzon eventually became a superb, if idiosyncratic, fighter.

"Monzon was not spectacular," said Argentine journalist and Monzon chronicler Ernesto Cherquis Bialo. "He was not entertaining, nor fast, nor charismatic. He was tenacious, patient, instinctive. He was like a wild animal, stalking until the moment of the final attack." Trainer Gil Clancy, who would be in the opposing corner many times during the 1970s, once noted the peculiarities of Monzon's style. "Monzon is a very hard fighter to beat," Clancy said. "He doesn't look good, but he takes this little step backward all the time, which tends to make you lunge. . . ." By making opponents lunge, Monzon kept them off balance. "He's terribly effective. It's very hard to establish a rhythm against him."

Boxing, Monzon once said, was like breathing. The key was to be comfortable in the ring, to control everything. If he wanted the pace to speed up, he'd speed it up. If he wanted it to slow down, he'd slow it down. He never watched film of opponents or studied their styles; he left such things to Brusa. "My opponents don't know how to fight me," Monzon said, "because I am unique." He began telling rivals, *You've never fought anyone like Monzon because there is only one Monzon!*

By the mid-1960s, Monzon already dripped with the arrogance that Hugh McIlvanney described as "profound confidence, the conviction that he has the animal authority to dominate almost any man they put in front of him."

Monzon also developed a tactic of starting a fight slowly, almost sleepily, and gradually increasing his punch output. It was like watching a machine warming up. His use of footwork was underrated; no matter where he stepped in the ring, Monzon was in position to fire his right cross from almost any angle. He was also adept at leaning on the ropes to avoid punishment, something similar to Ali's famous "rope-a-dope" strategy. (Monzon would actually claim that he, not Ali, had invented the trick.) Other aspects of Monzon's style were comparable to Ali's, particularly his use of the right lead, his flicking jab, his pacing, his tendency to "arm punch" rather than standing flat-footed to generate power, and his manner of leaning back and away from opponents. The difference was that Ali always looked graceful. Monzon was less picturesque, but no less effective. Monzon in the ring was like an uneducated man reciting a sonnet by Shakespeare; the delivery was raw, but the beauty was there if you paid attention.

# Luna Park 1965–69

By 1965 Monzon was fighting regularly at Luna Park in Buenos Aires.

Described ad nauseam as the Madison Square Garden of Argentina, the stadium covered most of a city block near the Buenos Aires waterfront. The famous venue saw everything from sports events to Nazi rallies and was known as the site where future Argentine president Juan Peron met his future wife, Eva. Its lush art deco design was somewhat offset by an intimidating iron fence that separated the cheap seats from the more expensive, its pointed prongs dividing the haves from the have-nots.

Luna Park's owner and boxing promoter, Juan Carlos "Tito" Lectoure, booked Monzon frequently. On February 1, 1966, Monzon challenged Argentina's middleweight champion, Jorge Fernandez, the so-called "Torito de Pompeya." In a major upset, Monzon won by decision to claim the Argentine title. Beating Fernandez was Monzon's greatest triumph thus far, proof of how he'd improved.

In between his Luna Park appearances, Monzon fought in less than glamorous locations, usually against weak opponents, including some who had never won a bout. Yet these easy nights endeared Monzon to the folks in the outer provinces. In a way, Monzon was undertaking an old-fashioned exhibition tour, bringing his name to places that didn't usually host boxing, including some of the country's poorest areas.

Lectoure, however, had a problem to solve. The Buenos Aires fans had adored Fernandez. They saw Monzon as a hick and occasionally booed him. Carlos Losauro pointed out years later that when Monzon fought at Luna Park in the 1960s, "the stadium was half empty." The reason, Losauro reckoned, was that Monzon was still considered just another boxer from "the pile."

A plan was formed to match Monzon against an American. Lectoure felt the Buenos Aires fans might never love Monzon, but, if given a choice between Monzon and an American, they'd have to cheer the native son. The idea nearly backfired.

Lectoure's choice was a little known African American fighter from Philadelphia named Bennie Briscoe. Sporting a modest record of 19-4, Briscoe stunned the Luna Park crowd on May 6, 1967, by holding Monzon to a ten-round draw. The bout became the stuff of minor legend, with Briscoe returning to America and claiming he'd been robbed of a victory by Argentine judges. "Briscoe is tough," Monzon said. "He makes you work."

Monzon went back to gorging on Argentine fighters, earning the championship of South America with another decision win over Fernandez. Starting in 1968, a ragtag succession of Americans were brought in for Monzon to fight in Buenos Aires, including Doug Huntley, Johnny Brooks, Charley Austin, Harold Richardson, Tom Bethea, and Eddie Pace. Monzon defeated them all, sometimes impressively, sometimes not. He was still maturing, still honing his style. The Americans liked to crowd him, while he wanted to use his long arms and box from a distance. "I didn't think he was so special at the time but I think he was still developing," Huntley told *The Ring* in 2015. "He just got better and better and better until he became a great fighter."

Then came the bout with Benvenuti, the championship, and the uproar that followed Monzon for the rest of his life.

Returning from Rome and landing by plane at the Ezeiza Airport in Buenos Aires was an emotional moment for the usually icy Monzon. A crowd of well-wishers had gathered to welcome the new champion home. He wrote in *My True Life*, "When I stuck my head out the window and saw the euphoric people in Ezeiza I thought: I exist, I am someone, I exist. . . ."

◆ ◆ ◆

On May 8, 1971, Monzon was in Monte Carlo for a rematch with Benvenuti. Before an audience that included royalty and international celebrities, plus coverage in America by ABC's *Wide World of Sports*, Benvenuti's corner stopped the bout at 1:05 of the third round. Benvenuti protested, but he'd been knocked down twice and couldn't cope with Monzon's roughhouse style. Benvenuti would say that Monzon was "big like a basketball player, and his success comes from bringing that right hand down on the back of your head."

While Benvenuti argued with his corner about the stoppage, Monzon surveyed the moneyed crowd. They were his now, as if he'd won not only Benvenuti's championship, but also the glamour. Monzon's only concern was the dull ache in his right hand. He had developed arthritis in his mighty weapon, an occupational hazard for heavy punchers. As had been Monzon's habit in recent years, he'd asked to be shot up with novocaine prior to the bout. Though this helped numb the pain, the needle had been dirty; his hand would grow dangerously infected and would require constant care for the remainder of his career. Monzon had finally reached the pinnacle of his profession, but had already begun to rot.

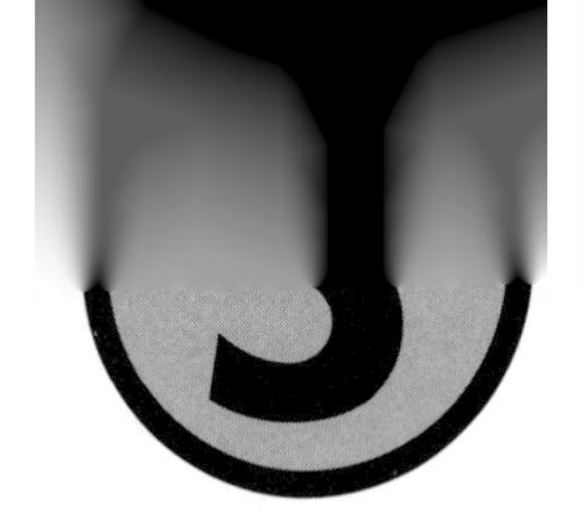

# Champion

In between his two bouts with Benvenuti, Monzon was back in Argentina for a trio of nontitle fights. The first was a homecoming at Luna Park just four weeks after winning the championship. Looking for an easy night, he was matched again with American journeyman Charley Austin. Monzon crushed him at 2:09 of the second round with what the United Press called "a tremendous right cross." Domingo Guerrero and Roy Lee, soft opponents brought in to face Monzon in Salta and Santa Fe, fared no better, each leveled by Monzon in the second round.

The new champion even returned to his old hometown of San Javier. He hadn't been there in years, but when he saw how the place had improved, he felt disappointed. He'd wanted to be the rich guy speeding through town in his own shiny car, with the poor people looking on in envy. Instead, he arrived to see that San Javier had been modernized. Denied his chance to be the prodigal son, he went to a bar and spent the day drinking.

Rumors spread that Monzon was being courted to fight in New York, but his next title defense would see him back in Luna Park to face Emile

Griffith, a former champion in two weight classes and a future Hall of Famer. On September 25, 1971, Monzon handled Griffith for most of thirteen rounds before finishing him off at 2:58 of the fourteenth.

"The toughest man I ever fought was Emile Griffith," Monzon would say. "He knows all the tricks and can make you do things you don't want to do."

The fight was praised by *Boxing Illustrated* as "a fast paced, exciting affair, almost worthy of the fantastic publicity that the Argentine press had lavished on it." Indeed, the contest had been hyped to the skies by Lectoure for being the first world middleweight championship bout held in South America. The massive event allegedly set a record gate, something in the vicinity of $130,000, small by American standards but enormous for Argentina. It also broke the existing attendance record at Luna Park, with a reported 21,350 people filling the venue. During the week before the fight, approximately 15,000 turned out in the rain simply to watch Monzon spar.

By now, Monzon had caught the eye of America. *The Ring* magazine chose his first bout with Benvenuti as Fight of the Year. Ted Carroll, known for his detailed illustrations for *The Ring*, prepared a full-page drawing of Monzon for an upcoming issue. Carroll wrote in the accompanying story, "There is a growing awareness that he may be a great one." New York newspapers included coverage of Monzon right next to articles about the Yankees and the Knicks, while *Sports Illustrated* fitted Monzon stories in between tales of famous French skiers and British trap shooters.

The early coverage of Monzon played him up as a good Catholic, a loyal father and husband, a devotee of the Virgin of Guadalupe, a simple man who overcame poverty to become, as Brusa declared, a figure of "national importance." More than one article stated dreamily that Monzon had never been a street fighter. In actuality, he had often fought in the streets and had already accumulated an impressive police record that would eventually total more than forty arrests. Promoter

Rodolfo Sabbatini would say in regard to Monzon, "It's not true when they say the best fighters come from ghettos. The best ones come from jail."

The hardscrabble childhood was traditional fodder for boxing stories, and Monzon played the role well. "I went from the gutter to the world title," he told *The Ring*. "I have reached a goal. But I am not satisfied. I've got to be paid for the many rough fights I went through for peanuts." Carefully conceived press releases described him as a regular guy who loved to go hunting and fishing, enjoyed movies, and was absolutely devoted to his young son, Abel.

What stands out about these early stories was the way Monzon was photographed to look like a stylish Latin pop star, usually in a long leather coat, with plenty of gold jewelry. Argentina's *El Grafico* treated Monzon like a model, featuring him in regular photo spreads. The reason: Monzon didn't look like other fighters of the day.

Seeing Monzon for the first time, particularly if you'd been raised on the bent-nosed pugs of the past, was an arresting experience. The way he left sportswriters reaching for words best implies what an astonishing presence Carlos Monzon must have been. Hugh McIlvanney once covered a Monzon bout and went on about the new champion's "handsome head" and his "high, molded cheekbones"—strange points to bring up in a boxing story. Bert Randolph Sugar stopped his usual flurry of puns to note that Monzon possessed the "reserved looks of a matinée idol . . . and a remarkable body that could serve as a model for Hollywood beefcake pictures." According to writer Mark Kram, Monzon was "a perfectly shaped middleweight, tall with long arms and with style running through every sinew up to his dramatic Belmondo face." Dave Anderson of the *New York Times* once wrote that Monzon "had the smoldering appearance of a volcano about to erupt." Edwin Shrake of *Sports Illustrated* wrote that Monzon had the "graceful, slightly swaggering walk of a man who likes his body" and a "brooding, sensual, vaguely dangerous look. . . ." A BBC announcer once referred to Monzon as "the handsome brute," while various journalists compared him to such rugged Hollywood stars as Anthony Quinn, Jack Palance, and Charles Bronson.

But if reporters were impressed with Monzon's screen-test-ready cheekbones, there was less enthusiasm about his fighting skill. When he'd first won the title, there was praise for his unusual style, the way he waited to strike, as one writer put it, with the patience of a sniper. As time passed, however, there was a tendency to point out his advantages in size, and little else. Remarks trickled in from English-speaking commentators during Monzon's bouts that he was "crude but effective" and "awkward but gets the job done." British reporter Reg Gutteridge described Monzon as having "little ring grace. He clubs as if wearing a Roman cestus on his fist." In the same article, Gutteridge pegged Monzon as "basically a stand-up fighter who hits tomahawk style." By 1975, Monzon was described in *Sports Illustrated* as "sloppy," with "no leverage nor the slightest notion of how to achieve it." Most damning, perhaps, was Kram's assertion that Monzon was "not a legend," but "a mere footnote, the product of Latin generosity and emotion."

And on it went over the next few years, with reporters gushing about his looks but rarely appreciating his ring work.

No wonder Monzon hated the press. "They are hoping I lose," he once said. "Even in Argentina."

◆ ◆ ◆

Monzon finished 1971 with a December bout at Luna Park against American journeyman Fraser Scott. In a nontitle event, Scott quit after the second round with a bruised rib.

In all, Monzon's first year as champion had been remarkable. It had been good enough, in fact, that barely any notice was given to Monzon being arrested twice that year, once in August for his part in a restaurant brawl, and again in September when he hit a man with his car. These were considered trifling matters, as was a domestic spat that resulted in a mysterious trip to an emergency room. Brusa did such a good job of keeping the press at bay that it wasn't known if it was Monzon or Mercedes who had needed treatment. Still, it was impossible for people to not notice Mercedes occasionally sported a bruised cheek or some other telltale sign of abuse.

There is little doubt that Monzon was already exhibiting the violence toward Mercedes that, as he later admitted, he inflicted on all of the women in his life. There were stories that Mercedes gave as good as she got, but this was probably an attempt by Monzon's admirers to soften his terrible reputation. A man can't be a wife batterer if the wife occasionally breaks a bottle over his head, or so the thinking went.

The image being created in the press, that of the glamorous boxing champion basking in newfound fame and wealth, created enough smoke around Monzon to deflect most public scrutiny. But had anyone known he wasn't the ideal family man presented in the press, it's doubtful they would've stepped in to keep Monzon off the tragic path he was treading.

Carlos Monzon was, in the early 1970s, a certified star with all the money he could've hoped for, but this didn't help with his temper. In fact, it may have made things worse.

Still, his reputation for cruelty, which was becoming known, didn't stop women from seeking his attention. They saw a fashionable, charming athlete—a man they wanted for themselves, not caring that he was already married—who seemed to glow like a movie star, with a broad smile that promised a good time. This wasn't the standard abuser of women, not some pathetic little man who took out his frustrations on his wife. The champion just didn't fit the stereotype they'd come to expect.

Yet, in many ways, Monzon was the typical wife abuser. He was obsessed with control; he had an evil temper; he drank too much. Though he never described his father beating his mother, he did mention once to a journalist that Roque used a whip on the Monzon boys if they misbehaved. Most domestic violence experts agree that wife batterers such as Monzon most likely saw their father abuse their mother. In the close confines of the family shack in San Javier, young Carlos probably witnessed many things he kept to himself. Granted, not all boys who see violence in their family go on to beat their wife. But somehow, in between daydreams about the Durango Kid, Monzon grew up thinking it was perfectly fine to smash a woman across the teeth.

In later years it was important for those who idolized Monzon, like his actor friend Alain Delon, to describe him as just a typical man of his time, place, and status. "What man hasn't hit his wife?" Delon once said in defense of Monzon. Mercedes would say that she did the only thing she could when Monzon attacked her: She defended herself. In Argentina's male-dominated society of the time, Mercedes saw nothing unusual in Monzon's behavior. Her own father had beaten her often, which was why she married so young, though she ended up with a man who brutalized her.

By the time Monzon was with Alicia Muniz, he was far more volatile than he'd been with Mercedes. He didn't mellow with age. "He has aggressive moments," Alicia said in a 1980 interview with *La Semana*. She described Monzon as "a boy who wants a toy. He craves it and, once he has it, destroys it." Alicia added, "When we just started dating, one night he told me not to fall in love with him because he was going to destroy me."

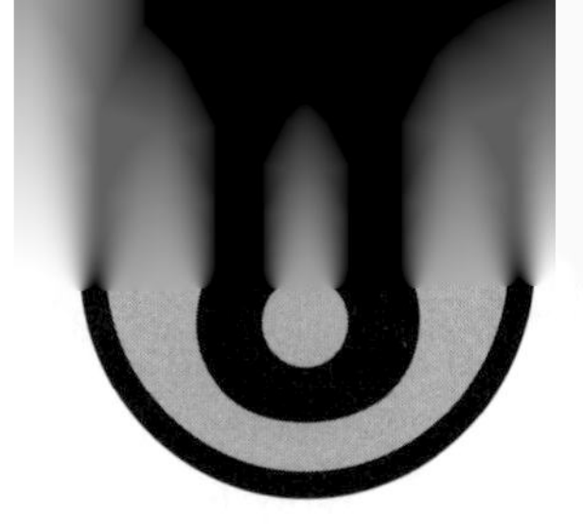

# Garbage and Miracles

In March of 1972, Monzon was back in Rome to defend the middleweight championship. The challenger was Denny Moyer, a slightly shopworn American contender who had turned professional in 1957. After scoring a quick knockdown of Moyer in the fifth round, Monzon was inexplicably declared the winner by referee Lorenzo Fortunato. Outraged by the stoppage, the crowd of 16,000 resumed their tradition of throwing garbage at the ring. A correspondent for *Boxing Illustrated* reported that a "ringside TV monitor was knocked out by a bread roll the length of a vaulting pole."

Monzon shrugged the evening off. "It's not my fault," he said.

Three months later Monzon was in Paris to fight Jean-Claude Bouttier, France's latest middleweight hope. Bouttier owned an impressive record of 56-3-1, but anyone at ringside that June night could see he was nervous. The AP reported that Bouttier was "white as chalk when he came into the ring . . . his eyes popping in a hyperthyroid stare."

Bouttier may have been moved by the magnitude of the event. It took place at Colombes Stadium, an honored venue built for the 1924 Paris

Olympics with seating for forty-five thousand. Though it drew considerably less than capacity, the fight reportedly set a financial record for a French sporting event. With the roar of his countrymen in his ears, Bouttier strolled down the aisle accompanied by blasting trumpets and waving flags. Bouttier later described his jitters. "I felt like I was in a tunnel," he said. "I couldn't think."

At least one reporter claimed Bouttier's eyes were moist with tears.

For all of his nerves, Bouttier put up a reasonable fight. During the sixth he suffered a knockdown, but he rose to his feet and charged at Monzon, his frenzied attack bringing cheers from the French audience. "He's a tough little cookie," ABC's Howard Cosell said of Bouttier. Bouttier wasn't boxing so much as flailing his arms, doing enough to keep Monzon leery. At one point he even wrestled Monzon to the canvas. After the round, which *Sports Illustrated* said "should be preserved in a war museum," Bouttier's confidence was high.

The next few rounds were less frantic sequels to the demented sixth, the crowd cheering every flutter of Bouttier's gloves. Gradually, Bouttier found himself fighting for survival. By the tenth round his left eye was swelling shut and he was exhausted. At one point he could do nothing more than lean on Monzon; it looked like the champion was propping Bouttier up, unsure of how to knock him out. Early in the twelfth Monzon landed a crushing right hand to Bouttier's head that shook the entire ring. Bouttier staggered sideways but somehow stayed upright. By the end of the round he was too tired to continue. Bouttier's manager, Jean Bretonnel, stopped the bout. "I lost to a great champion," Bouttier said.

If fights were reviewed like Broadway plays, the lukewarm reactions to Monzon's win would result in a short run at the box office. The theme of the coverage was that he was simply a bigger man, and Bouttier had seemed scared. Monzon retained the title, but Bouttier and his sentimental French fans were the story.

◆ ◆ ◆

Two months later, Monzon scored an easy fifth-round knockout of Tom Bogs in Copenhagen, Denmark. Bouttier nodded knowingly from ringside. "Monzon," Bouttier said, "is a terrifying opponent, enormously powerful and ice-cold. Bogs learned that tonight."

In September, Monzon made a pilgrimage from Santa Fe to the small town of Vallecito—an eleven-hour trip over bad roads, speeding all the way—to visit the shrine of Difunta Correa, a Catholic hero from the San Juan province. An unofficial saint, Correa died during the Argentine civil war of the 1840s. According to legend, she was found with her still-alive infant feeding from her breast. Thousands visit her shrine every year and leave gifts. Among the mountain of tributes left at Correa's shrine, Monzon laid the trunks he'd worn in the Bogs fight.

October saw Monzon make a ten-hour trip to the province of Rio Negro to see the shrine of Ceferino Namuncurá, "The Lily of the Patagonia." A religious student who had died young in 1905, Namuncurá was the son of an Indian and held a special fascination for Argentina's indigenous people. In 2007, the Roman Catholic Church beatified Namuncurá after several Argentines claimed his intervention had cured them of diseases. In 1972, Monzon humbly left the boots he'd worn while beating Bouttier in France.

If Monzon sought divine assistance, it was likely because of his deteriorating right hand. The arthritis was a serious problem, but he wasn't ready to quit boxing. For the first Benvenuti fight, he'd made only $15,000. Now he was making nearly ten times that amount for each defense of his title. As he often said, a champion "has to make the juice."

He was also preparing to face a rival from his past: Bennie Briscoe.

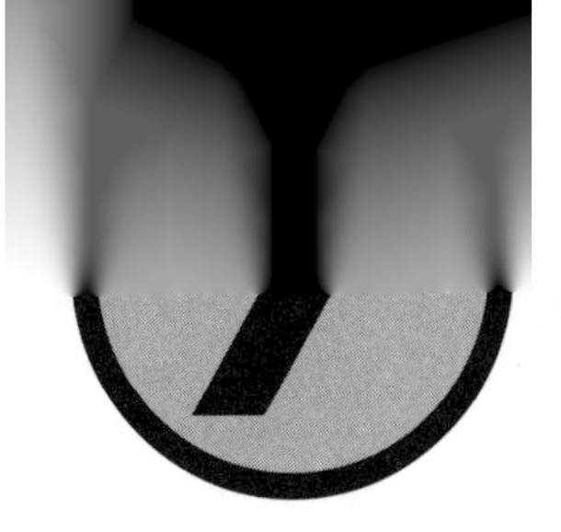

# Bad Bennie

Bennie Briscoe was such a badass that Monzon deliberately changed his style for their November 11, 1972, bout in Buenos Aires. To avoid Briscoe's brute strength, Monzon became a slash-and-move artist, slipping around the ring with surprising elegance, raking Briscoe with countershots and combinations. Briscoe finally caught Monzon in the ninth, landing a short right that stunned the champion and made him hold on. Other than that, and an instant in the fourteenth when Briscoe landed another good right, the night was Monzon's. He put on a gorgeous display of boxing and earned a unanimous fifteen-round decision. "Monzon is a great champion," Briscoe said. "He clearly won." Indeed, Monzon had painted a masterpiece.

"To me it proved Monzon's greatness because he was able to neutralize Bennie," said Briscoe's Philadelphia promoter, J Russell Peltz.

More than four decades later, the fight is still memorable for Peltz. "It was the first weigh-in I'd been to that turned into a mob scene. There were two or three thousand people, and a police barricade. I couldn't believe it. Then, for some reason Monzon took his finger and made circles around

Bennie's nipples. He was just being silly. Bennie would've punched a guy for doing that, but I think Bennie was intimidated by the situation. And in the fight, he was intimidated by the referee who kept warning him.

"I was in that corner when he hurt Monzon, and the entire first row, Sabbatini and those people, looked like they were going to swallow their cigarettes. And Monzon, I could see him clearly from where I sat; he looked like he might throw up. But who knows what would've happened if Bennie knocked him out. Maybe we wouldn't have gotten out of there."

The fight had been a kind of Argentine happening. Even Argentine president General Alejandro Lanusse got involved in the hype, inviting the fighters to have lunch with him at the presidential palace and posing with them for photos.

Yet this was also the fight that created some suspicion of Monzon in America, with stories of Argentine officials protecting their champion, even confiscating a jar of cut salve from Briscoe's corner, and forcing Briscoe's handlers to sit a full eight feet from the ring. Referee Victor Avendano was another point of controversy. Not only did the Argentine promoter employ him, but he'd once been spotted carrying Monzon's bag. "People said the officials were all working for Monzon, and the scoring was ridiculous. I don't think they gave Bennie the ninth when he had Monzon hurt," said Peltz. "But there was no doubt Monzon won."

The shame of the accusations was that Monzon hadn't needed protection. He fought a beautiful fight. Even Briscoe remained an admirer. "He was a very good fighter, tall and hard to hit," Briscoe said. "There weren't many guys who could box as well as Monzon." Monzon, not one to praise opponents, never missed a chance to compliment Briscoe. "My God," Monzon once said. "What a head of stone—and a big heart!"

As 1972 turned into 1973, Monzon presented himself to the world as a doting father and a proud family man. He'd also embarked on a sort of mad spending spree, determined to erase his past as a poor boy sleeping on the floor of a shack. He owned a 1,750-acre ranch in San Javier, complete with cattle, sheep, and horses, plus a collection of expensive firearms imported from Italy. He bought houses for his parents and his wife's parents. He owned eight apartments in Buenos Aires, and four in Santa Fe. He owned a Fiat 128, and a yellow and black Lutteral, a custom-made Argentine sports car with a klaxon horn (or, as it's better known, an "ahooga" horn). He was also building a new home in Santa Fe. He had closets filled with expensive suits, hundreds of custom-made shirts and neckties, and allegedly a pair of shoes for every day of the year.

To the outside world, Monzon had it all.

Then his wife shot him.

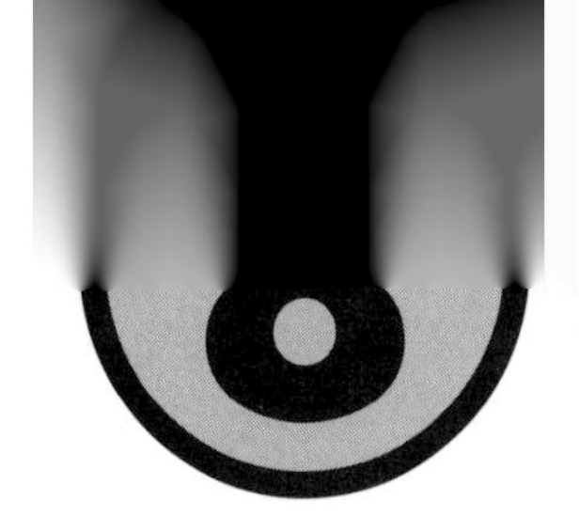

# Bullets

The report from Argentina: Monzon had accidentally shot himself.

On February 28, 1973, Monzon endured a two-hour operation to remove a bullet from his right forearm. He told the press that he was getting ready to go hunting when his .22-caliber revolver had slipped from his hand, "firing as it hit the floor." The *New York Daily News* joked, "Everybody is taking a shot at middleweight champ Carlos Monzon these days."

The story was soon out that two bullets had found their way into Monzon courtesy of Mercedes, his wife of nearly a dozen years. By now she was better known in Argentina by her nickname, "Pelusa," which was Spanish for "Fluff." Mercedes played along with the false story at first. As Monzon underwent surgery at a San Miguel hospital, Mercedes posed for photographers, smiling sweetly. "I've always told Carlos to be careful of his weapons," she said. "But . . . people think badly and try to make me responsible. It wasn't me. It was only an accident."

The police seemed satisfied with the "accident" story, which was odd since Monzon had actually been shot twice, once in the arm and once in the shoulder. A gun might discharge after being dropped, but to think it would go off twice—and hit a target—was ridiculous. But Monzon's standing in Argentina was such that the police acknowledged the story, or perhaps accepted some hush money to drop the investigation, even though neighbors told police that just prior to the gunshots being heard, Monzon and Mercedes had been seen brawling in the front yard of their home.

A story emerged that Mercedes shot Monzon after learning of his affair with another woman. Monzon's womanizing was a secret to no one—he and Mercedes would even adopt a child, Carlos Raul, whom many suspected was the result of one of Monzon's extramarital affairs.

Monzon didn't go for help, opting to sit around the house for a day—only Monzon would consider walking off a couple of bullets—but when Brusa learned what had happened, the trainer arranged for his champion to be taken to a hospital. By now, Brusa was experienced at running interference for Monzon. He was used to negotiating with commissioners, mediating between Monzon and Mercedes, and convincing journalists to ignore Monzon's frequent scandals. Gunshots were something new. Brusa faced the press with an amazingly calm demeanor, saying the injuries wouldn't hamper Monzon's scheduled rematch with Emile Griffith. What Brusa didn't report was that the second bullet was inoperable, and that the little slug would remain inside Monzon's shoulder. It would be there for the rest of his life, a small reminder of the damage his infidelities might bring.

While recuperating, Monzon received news from America that the Boxing Writers Association had chosen him as the recipient of the Edward J. Neil Trophy for Fighter of the Year. Along with the BWA accolade, both *Boxing Illustrated* and *The Ring* honored him as the top boxer of 1972 (*The Ring* recognizing Monzon and Muhammad Ali together). Yet, even as the accolades rolled in, Monzon was dealing with problems, and not just his wife's trigger finger.

First, making weight for fights had become a struggle. Monzon began his career as a middleweight, and now he had to starve himself to make the

160-pound limit. In 1973, there was no 168-pound class for him to join—the super middleweights wouldn't be established until the 1980s —and he never seriously considered a jump to light heavyweight. Chances are he didn't want to give up his height and reach advantages, which is what would've happened if he'd moved up to face the men of a heavier weight division. Also, a court case was pending regarding an assault charge from years earlier when Monzon had punched a photographer, Daniel Moreno.

Meanwhile, attendance for the Briscoe fight had been lower than anticipated, a mere seventeen thousand. The four thousand or so empty seats at Luna Park left Lectoure puzzled. What could Lectoure do if Monzon couldn't fill Luna Park with Briscoe as his opponent? Worse, there was growing gossip that opponents wouldn't fight Monzon in Argentina because of the preferential treatment he received.

As expected, the rematch with Griffith was postponed so Monzon could heal from his bullet wounds. When he felt fit, he agreed to a nontitle bout in Rome on May 5. Looking sluggish, Monzon stopped Cincinnati middleweight Roy Dale at 2:40 of the fifth round. The AP noted that Monzon was not only three and a half pounds over the middleweight limit, but looked "distracted, as many of his punches missed their mark."

The distraction had to do with the news Monzon received on the morning of the fight. His younger brother, Zacarias, had been murdered by a co-worker in the town of Paleda, sixty miles from Santa Fe. Brusa tried to keep the news from Monzon, but the champion had fought after receiving similar news in the past. On the eve of his first bout with Benvenuti, a brother-in-law died of natural causes, and on the eve of his fight with Moyer, his father-in-law was killed in a car crash.

Death was never far from Carlos Monzon.

He had a bullet in his body to prove it.

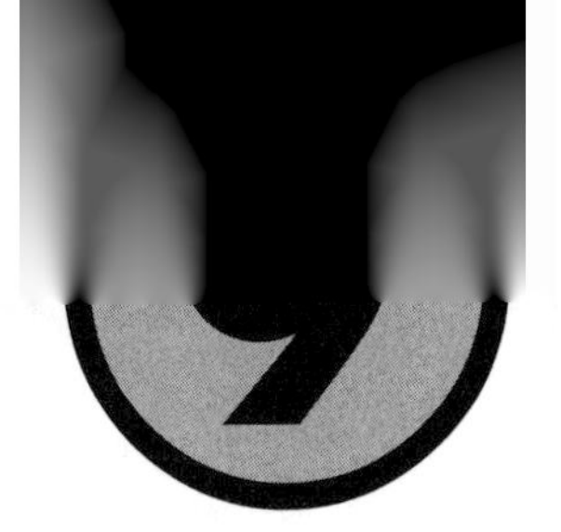

# Taking on the World

A drained and thin-looking Monzon was back in action four weeks later in Monaco for his June 2 rematch with Griffith. In front of a bored crowd of nine thousand, many of them in Monte Carlo for that weekend's Grand Prix, Monzon pawed his way to a dreary, fifteen-round decision win. He sulked after the bout, telling the press he had looked bad because dieting to make weight had stolen his strength. He added that he might retire rather than fight again in such a weakened state. Nino Benvenuti, serving as a commentator for Italian television, spoke for many when he panned Monzon's effort. "He did nothing," Benvenuti said. "Griffith made the fight."

Monzon's retirement talk didn't last long. There was already an offer for him to meet Bouttier again in France for $130,000.

On June 17, Monzon appeared in New York's Roosevelt Hotel ballroom to receive his Fighter of the Year award at the annual Boxing Writers Association dinner. The BWA was hosting a special "Salute to the Middleweights," with many boxing greats from previous decades in attendance. But if Monzon was supposed to ingratiate himself to the icons of the past, no one told him. He sat at the dais, sipping wine and sneering.

More than one journalist in attendance noticed Monzon's agitation. Columnist Bill Gallo described Monzon as "a petulant child." Dick Young of the *New York Daily News* commented that Monzon was "gauche" and "rude." Monzon refused to pose for photos, and was even disrespectful to Argentine consulate Rafael M. Vazquez, who had flown in for the occasion. When stand-up comic Mal Z. Lawrence was entertaining the crowd of four hundred, Monzon grew so bored that he threatened to leave, forcing Lawrence to cut his routine short. At another point in the evening, Monzon was so distressed that Vazquez, along with Argentine journalist Manolo Rodriguez, had to calm him down.

Nigel Collins, future editor of *The Ring* magazine, remembered his own interaction with Monzon that night. "Bennie Briscoe, Russell Peltz, Quenzell McCall, and I took a train from North Philly to Manhattan to attend the BWA awards for 1972," Collins recalled. "After shaking hands with Jack Dempsey, I spotted Monzon standing alone off to one side. He looked magnificent in a tailor-made suit, but was stone-faced and gave off a haughty vibe. As I approached, he began to smile. I thought the smile was for me, but it wasn't. I didn't know Briscoe was close behind. The smile was for him. Monzon had great respect for Bennie and was legitimately happy to see him. I shook Monzon's hand and congratulated him. He just lowered his head slightly in response. Then I beat a hasty retreat so Carlos and Bennie could have a private chat. It was the only time I saw Monzon smile all evening.

"He was a prick, unless you were Bennie Briscoe."

In the future, some of his friends would claim Monzon was moody during this period because his personal life was out of control. He was juggling a harem of women, and trying to keep Mercedes from knowing. Sometimes they said he simply didn't like journalists. "If the press complains about me," Monzon said, "they ought to be in my shoes so they know what hell is like."

Cherquis Bialo felt Monzon had an aversion to reporters simply because he'd never adjusted to his level of fame. "He hadn't grown up as a person," Bialo said. "The public figure he had become was stronger than the individual; this generated problems with journalists and also with his personal relationships. It was difficult for him to understand the authorities, the press, the dignitaries of state. He had no facility to express what he felt, so he resorted to silence or gestures.

"Fame allowed him to meet well-known actors and beautiful women that he had only seen on television, but he was better off within his circle of friends, rather than out in public. Being famous made it difficult to avoid what was hardest for him: talking."

Regardless, his associates were constantly excusing his rudeness. "Don't mind it if Monzon doesn't seem to like you," a friend of his once told a reporter from *Sports Illustrated*. "He's that way with nearly everybody. The way he grew up as a poor kid on the streets, he never needed to know much about manners, and he doesn't trust many people."

Monzon's bad manners were becoming legendary. Gil Clancy, trainer of Griffith, recalled a time when Monzon's nasty personal habits were in full view. "We were staying at some luxury hotel in Italy with these gorgeous rugs," Clancy said. "He just spit on the floor." There were also reports of Monzon's son Abel blowing his nose on a hotel curtain, which Monzon laughingly encouraged. Argentine reporters accepted this as Monzon's way of striking back at the wealthy, who had always made him feel insignificant as a child.

Mercedes would say that money, more than anything else, had changed Monzon. "He thought that because he had money," she said, "he could take on the world."

"He was not arrogant in the beginning of his career," said Argentine journalist Carlos Irusta. "When I met him for first time, when he was not Argentine champion but only a contender, he was humble and quiet. But . . . I remember what a friend of mine told me a lot of years ago: 'People don't change . . . they only take off their mask.'"

Carlos Monzon defeats Jorge Fernandez at Luna Park in Buenos Aires for the Argentine middleweight title on September 3, 1966. *El Grafico/Getty Images*

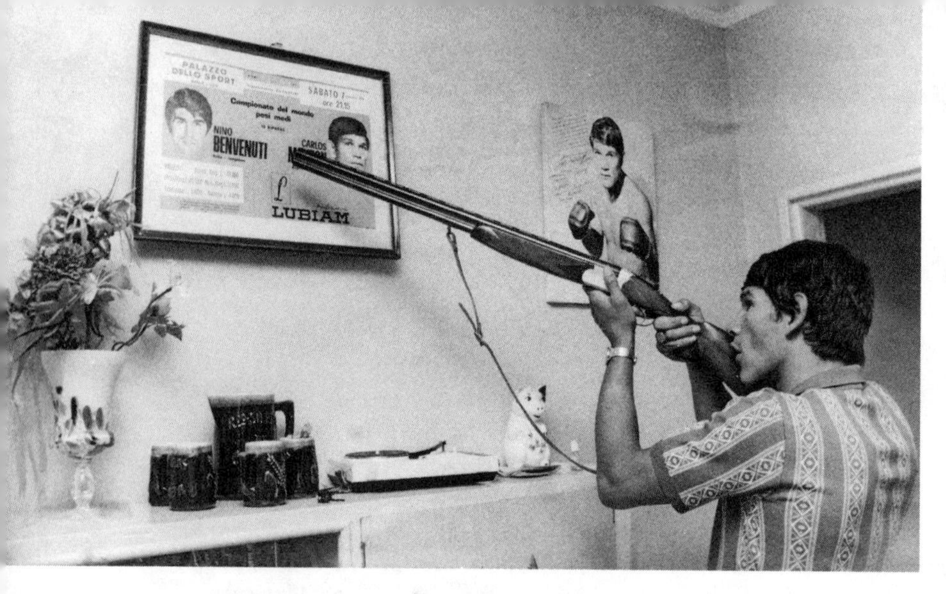


Monzon takes aim at a poster of his next opponent, Nino Benvenuti. *El Grafico/Getty Images*

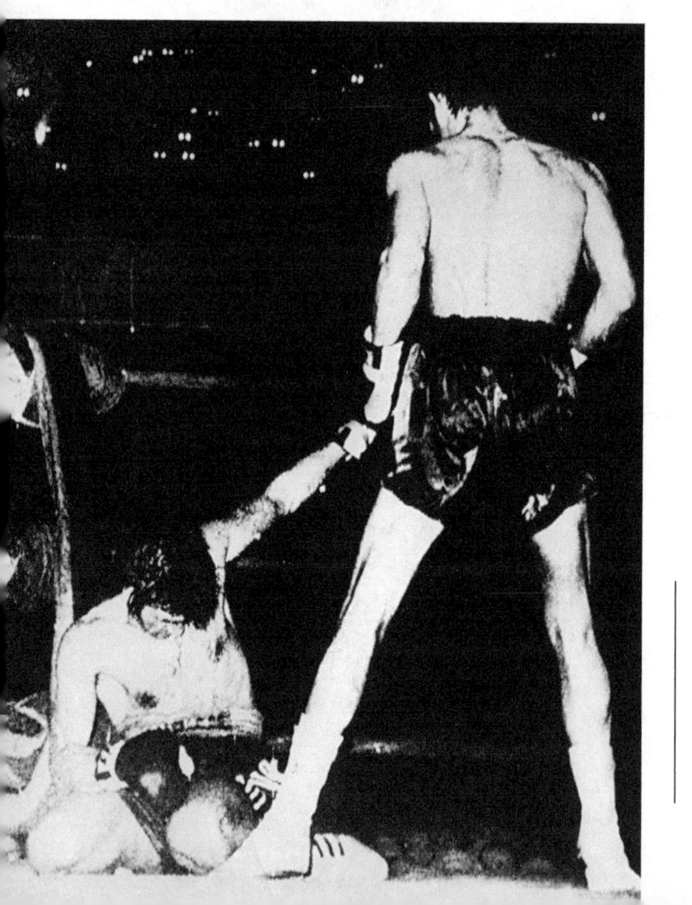

Monzon knocks out Benvenuti at 1:57 of round twelve to win the world middleweight title at the Palazzetto dello Sport in Rome on November 7, 1970. *El Grafico/Getty Images*

With the championship comes celebrity. Monzon at Moulin Rouge in Paris, 1974. *El Grafico/Getty Images*

*El Grafico*, a popular Argentine magazine, often had Monzon pose in exotic locations. Here he is with a lion in Monte Carlo in 1977. *El Grafico/Getty Images*

Carlos Monzon kisses his first wife, Mercedes, at a victory celebration. *El Grafico/Getty Images*

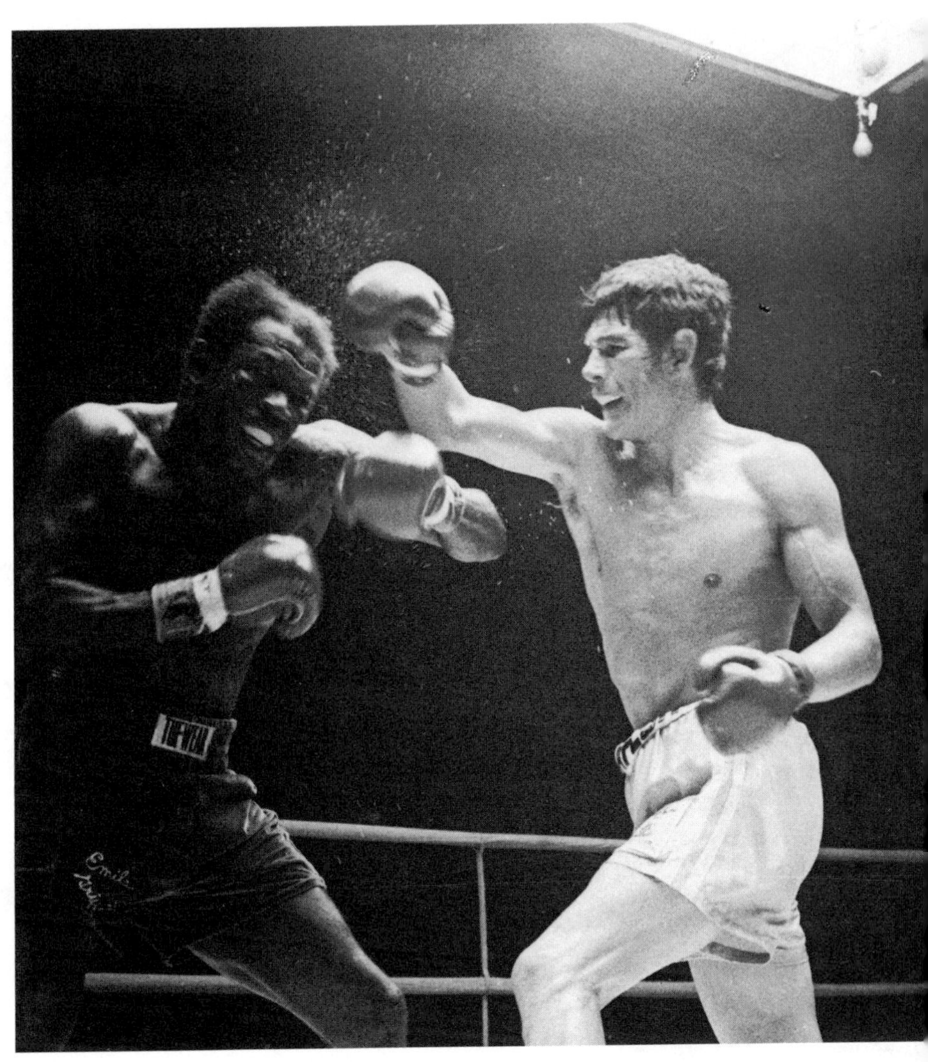


Monzon's first title defense was a fourteenth-round TKO victory over Emile Griffith. The fight was a major event in Argentina, drawing a huge crowd. *El Grafico/Getty Images*

Monzon, momentarily stunned by Bennie Briscoe, went on to win a fifteen-round decision in their fight at Luna Park in Buenos Aires on November 11, 1972. *El Grafico/Getty Images*

Monzon with his son, Abel, and two-time opponent, Jean-Claude Bouttier. *Gamma-Rapho/Getty Images*

Monzon with actress Susana Gimenez.
Many felt that she was the love of his life.
*Gamma-Rapho/Getty Images*

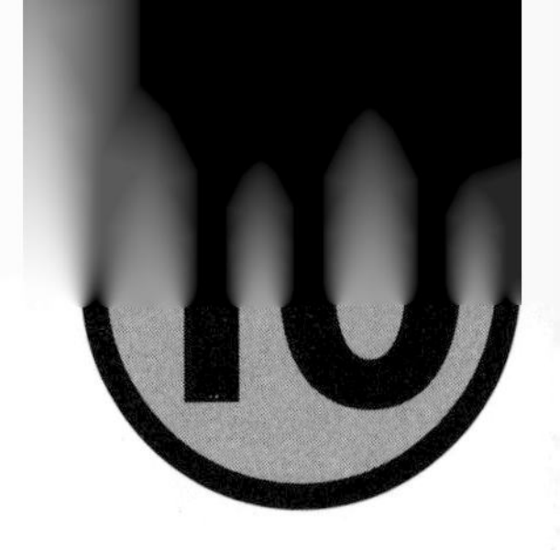

# A Glass Full of Piss

On August 7, 1973, Monzon did something he'd never done before: He celebrated his birthday. He did it up grandly, renting the Lebanese Syrian club in Santa Fe. With Mercedes and the children at his side, Monzon stood majestically in a blue suit and greeted every one of his hundred or so guests with a hug and a kiss and a beaming smile. An enormous cake with thirty-one candles was wheeled out. It was all quite childlike and strangely innocent. Monzon explained that his parents had been too poor to indulge their children with parties. He turned to Juan Carlos Lectoure and said, "It is the first time in my life that I'm going to blow out the candles on a birthday cake. . . ."

In late September, Monzon was back in France for a second bout with Jean-Claude Bouttier. Twelve thousand fans at the Roland Garros Tennis Stadium in Paris saw Monzon knock Bouttier down three times on his way to a unanimous decision win. Despite generally good notices, some thought Monzon was showing his age. "The Monzon of this fight was far from the champion he used to be," said a correspondent from *The Ring* magazine.

Monzon vowed that his next fight would be his last, citing Cuban-born welterweight champion Jose Napoles, Australia's Tony Mundine, and Colombia's Rodrigo Valdes as possible opponents. Perhaps to fulfill his narcissistic need to dominate, the opponent chosen was the smallest, Napoles. Fighting a smaller opponent, whom many believed was older than the "thirty-three" on his boxing license, would allow Monzon to revive his image as a destroyer. He wanted this to be his last fight, and wanted to be sure of a win. But just as journalists began grinding out stories about welterweights chasing the middleweight title, the bout was postponed when Monzon came down with the flu. He spent the end of 1973 under a doctor's care, unable to eat. It was a dramatic shift from the end of 1972, when *The Ring* magazine named him Fighter of the Year (along with Muhammad Ali). Indeed, 1973 had been difficult for Monzon: He'd been shot; his brother was killed; and he hadn't been impressive in his three ring appearances.

Adding to Monzon's end-of-the-year blues was the WBC's decision to strip him of one of his two title belts. Since beating Benvenuti, Monzon had been recognized as champion by the World Boxing Council and the World Boxing Association. Because of Monzon's decision to fight Napoles rather than the WBC's top middleweight contender, Valdes, the WBC made moves to strip Monzon and replace him. The box-off would feature Valdes against Bennie Briscoe.

The WBC was also angry with Monzon for his refusal to take part in a postfight drug test after beating Bouttier. Not only had he not left a urine sample, but he refused to pay the $5,000 fine levied by the European Boxing Union. As he'd been doing for years, Monzon was putting himself above people and doing things his way.

In December, Monzon lost control of his car on a Santa Fe highway and hit a light pole. Aside from some minor bruises to his legs, he wasn't badly hurt. Typically, he learned nothing. He had another car accident a few weeks later in Buenos Aires.

There was one positive note to end the year. It was announced on December 28 that Monzon had been cast in a film titled *La Mary*. Shooting would begin in Buenos Aires immediately after Monzon fought Napoles.

The actor with the movie-star looks was actually going to be a movie star.

◆ ◆ ◆

Monzon demolished Napoles. As expected, the welterweight champion was clearly too small, giving away nearly five inches in height, four in reach, and six pounds in weight. Though Napoles landed a few good punches early, Monzon's size was too much for him. By the fifth round, Napoles seemed frozen in a classic boxer's stance, his head bent slightly forward like a doomed man approaching a guillotine, while Monzon pounded on him. One of Monzon's punches, wrote the *New York Times*, was delivered with "the ceremonious air of a man driving the final spike in a railroad track." One ringside reporter described the one-sided beating as "horrifying."

The bout took place in a circus tent pitched in front of a subway entrance in Puteaux, Hauts-de-Seine, labeled by the AP as a "forlorn Paris suburb." Napoles garnered most of the prefight press. He was the brave underdog, while Monzon was once again portrayed as the surly heel. Monzon spent the week before the fight pummeling sparring partners. He allegedly didn't smile until the night of the contest when he was introduced to the old French ring legend, Georges Carpentier.

More than eleven thousand fans showed up on February 9 to see the mismatch, not put off by the many cynical columns written about the circus atmosphere. When Napoles returned to his corner after round six, his right eyebrow was hemorrhaging. Napoles's team immediately stopped the fight and accused Monzon of using his thumb to blind their fighter. Napoles said the thumbing didn't matter. "I surely could not have beaten him," he said. Monzon said of the fight, "It was almost too easy."

Despite many problems with publicity and broadcast arrangements, the event blazed with a kind of kitschy flair. The bout's promoter of record was popular French actor Alain Delon, who had become friends with Monzon. Delon's special touches included a newly commissioned piece of music for the ring walks—all screeching trumpets and crashing cymbals—with two roving spotlights breaking the blackness of nightfall. When the lights came up, ringsiders could see that *Playboy* magazine had purchased ad space on the corner ring posts, which were adorned with the magazine's iconic bunny. As for Monzon, he was said to have made $175,000 for the bout, plus a percentage of television and radio rights throughout Argentina, Europe, and America. He'd also rented space on his trunks to Fernet Branca, a popular Italian liqueur. This combination of big money, martial music, and tawdry spectacle was pure Monzon; the boy who once hunted swamp rodents had arrived on the big stage as a vehicle for vulgar advertising and a cheesy brass section. He probably thought a *Playboy* model was included in his rider.

Monzon, again, avoided the postfight drug test. There were witnesses who claimed he'd actually left the site of the fight in a limousine while still in his boxing gear. He changed clothes at his hotel and was later found celebrating in a local nightclub. When officials weaved through the party crowd and demanded he submit to a drug test, he flew into a typical Monzon rage. The story wavers here: Monzon either produced a urine sample that he'd apparently been carrying around since before the fight, or merely handed over a bar glass full of piss. Bernard Restour, president of the French Boxing Federation, threatened Monzon and Brusa with heavy fines and suggested Monzon be suspended from fighting in France. Lectoure, now acting as Monzon's business manager, claimed Monzon's dressing quarters—a circus trailer without running water or working toilet—hadn't been adequate. In the postfight chaos, Monzon simply left without a test.

Begrudgingly, Monzon agreed to provide a urine sample at his hotel the next morning.

Decades later, Cherquis Bialo would tell Argentina's Radio 2 that Monzon had skipped the drug test because he feared his urine would have traces of the novocaine that had been shot into his hand. According to Bialo, the sample eventually turned in wasn't Monzon's urine at all, but a mixture of Lectoure's, two little boys', and Bialo's. Such was Monzon's grip on his home nation that even a journalist would put aside his integrity and pee in a cup for him.

The bout was a financial success, but one critic after another declared that the victory showed only that Monzon was too big to be messing around with welterweights. The AP called the fight "an esthetic disappointment."

If Monzon heard the comments, he probably didn't care.

He had a movie to make.

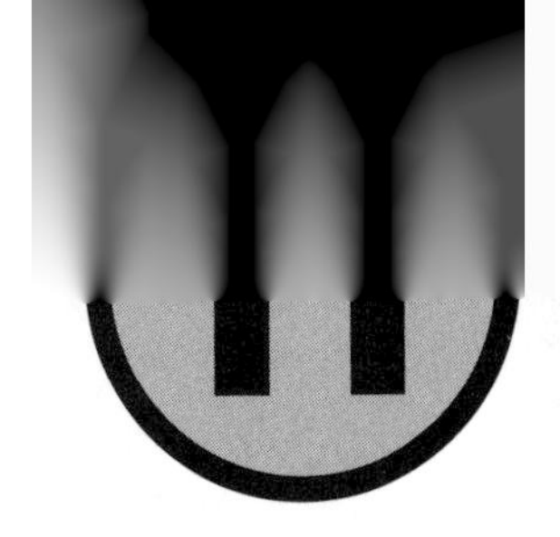

# The Boxer and the Beauty

When Monzon met Susana Gimenez during a publicity shoot for *La Mary* in early 1974, he thought she was a bit thin but was impressed with her personality. She had exactly what he was looking for in his quest to improve his image. Though Mercedes had been a loyal wife and mother to his children, Monzon now required a more glamorous woman at his side, a woman befitting a champion and movie star. A little dazzler who was already a show business veteran at twenty-eight, Maria Susana Gimenez Aubert came from a tough background and already had a daughter from a failed marriage. But with incredible ambition she had carved a niche for herself in television and movies, and had appeared in enough sexy advertising campaigns to earn a reputation as Argentina's "shock girl." When they met for the first time, photographers encouraged Monzon to give Susana a friendly kiss, right in front of her boyfriend, Héctor Cavallero. A major player in Argentine show business, Cavallero had helped arrange for Monzon to be in the movie. Now he could only stand back and watch the crazy heat between Susana and the boxer from Santa Fe.

The role of "Cholo" in *La Mary* seemed an unlikely way to kick off Monzon's movie career. There had already been talk that Monzon would be the James Bond of South America, but in *La Mary* he would not only be asked to trade in his custom-made clothes for a period suit from the 1940s, but he'd be playing the husband of a disturbed woman who claims to have psychic powers. Susana had the showy role. In fact, it was Susana who had read the *La Mary* novel and pushed for it to be made into a film.

Casting Monzon was a gamble. Even Susana doubted he could memorize lines or give them any meaning. Of his limited education, Monzon would often say he was smart enough to sign a contract and didn't need to know anything else. Still, the film's producers were made nervous by his near inability to read. Monzon had recently been invited to Paris to receive an award and couldn't even remember the simple phrase "Merci beaucoup." Instead, he blurted out "Pipi cuckoo." Director Daniel Tinayre, a well-regarded Argentine-French filmmaker who had been in the movie business since the 1930s, told Susana and the movie financiers not to worry. He planned to use a voice double on Monzon, a standard practice in Argentine movies. All that mattered, Tinayre said, was that Monzon looked good and he was famous. Tinayre's hunch was correct.

Movie buffs consider *La Mary* a minor gem in Argentine cinema, and in 2014 it was remastered and released on DVD for its fortieth anniversary. In its time, the sex scenes between Monzon and Susana were so highly charged that a newly formed right-wing terrorist group—the Argentine Anticommunist Alliance, or "Triple A,"—threatened to kill both of them, along with Tinayre. Fortunately, Triple A kept busy that year by assassinating politicians and priests instead.

Terrorists aside, the real story to come out of *La Mary* was the romance between Monzon and Susana. Each was smitten with the other. Monzon would tell friends that he couldn't keep his hands off of Susana all during filming. As for Susana, after many years in the company of effete Argentine actors and producers, meeting Monzon was probably akin to meeting Tarzan. That is, a Tarzan who was rich and had his own hideaway pad for entertaining women, complete with a Jacuzzi. Monzon and Susana took turns impressing each other with their money and status. Monzon had found a woman who was not just his equal in terms of ambition, but a suitable partner for the next phase of his career. "I really believe she was the love of his life," said Cherquis Bialo. "He wanted to better himself for her."

Their early days together were full of intrigue and drama, one secret rendezvous after another. Sometimes they would sneak around in disguises, to fool the press. But the one person who wasn't fooled had already put a bullet in Monzon's shoulder.

Mercedes eventually confronted Susana at the premiere of *La Mary*. Defending a marriage that was already threadbare, Mercedes promised to shoot Susana in the head if she didn't stay away from her husband. When Monzon heard about the encounter, he told Mercedes that their marriage was over. He tried to keep things civil because of their children, and continued living with Mercedes even as he was seeing Susana. However, constantly seeing newspaper photos of her husband with Susana drove Mercedes to file for divorce. Monzon's violence had never been enough to end the marriage. It was his unfaithfulness that did it.

In the coming years, Mercedes remained supportive of Monzon, no matter the scandals or criminal acts that involved him. At one point she even told the press that if he ever decided to return to her, she would forgive him and take him back. They were linked, she said, not only because of their children, but because they both came from the same obscurity. As she turned increasingly to religion and presented herself as a battered but unbowed survivor of a difficult marriage, reporters would often consult with Mercedes on issues concerning her ex-husband. They'd always be surprised to see that her home served as a shrine to Monzon, gigantic framed posters and old trophies covering every inch of the main rooms.

Meanwhile, Monzon and his glamorous new girlfriend were now free and clear to be together. "It was a great passion, a great love. Madness," Susana said in an interview forty-five years later.

One afternoon as they strolled around Mar del Plata, reveling in the success of *La Mary* and their blossoming romance, Susana noticed some penguins on the beach. Enchanted by the funny birds, Susana said that she wished she could pet one of them. Wishing to please, Monzon picked up a rock and smashed a penguin on the head. Then he hoisted the bird to his shoulders and brought it to Susana. She took one look at the nearly dead animal and screamed. "You told me you wanted to touch him," Monzon said, oblivious to what he had done. It must have been an amusing tableaux: the sexy blonde actress in shock, the ignorant boxer standing before her, holding in his arms a dazed and bloody penguin, a symbol of his love and devotion.

◆ ◆ ◆

The time was right for Lectoure to bring Monzon back to Luna Park. With a successful movie to his credit, as well as the demolition of Jose Napoles, Monzon was the hottest he'd been since winning the championship. His challenger for the grand homecoming would be Tony Mundine, a twenty-three-year-old Australian contender who had bad-mouthed Monzon many times. After one of Mundine's verbal jabs, reporters looked to Monzon for a response. The champion smirked and said, "Ask him if he has seen *La Mary*."

The bout took place on October 5, 1974. Lectoure's biggest challenge was to work out a seating plan that would prevent Susana and Mercedes from bumping into each other. Other than that, Lectoure's job was easy. Luna Park was packed with more than twenty thousand roaring Argentines on hand to witness their famous champion's tenth title defense. Mundine had boasted before the bout that he'd be too young and strong for the aging titlist, but if Monzon was slipping, he still had too much for the challenger. With ease, Monzon punished the younger man until he was declared the winner at 1:10 of the seventh round. The thunderous explosion of the crowd amazed Cherquis Bialo as Mundine was counted out. "It was," Bialo said, "the most memorable ten seconds in the history of Luna Park."

At the fight's conclusion, Monzon was raised in the air by admirers and carried out of the ring. As the Buenos Aires crowd filled the air with something like a war chant, Monzon blew kisses. After the bout, Monzon talked retirement. "I want to star in another film," he said. "You can't do that with a battered head."

The event was a financial success for Lectoure. It had drawn the biggest crowd for Monzon since the first Griffith bout, and showed that Monzon was still a star in Buenos Aires. He was, without a doubt, the greatest boxer the country had ever produced.

Neither the fighter nor his legion of fans knew that he would never again fight in Argentina.

◆ ◆ ◆

His triumphant return to Luna Park did nothing to dampen Monzon's temper. Just weeks after defeating Mundine, he attacked Mercedes and sent her to the hospital.

It happened during a birthday party for Abel. When Mercedes made a comment about Susana, Monzon reared back and punched her in the eye. She went to the hospital for stitches and learned she had a cracked superciliary arch. Since they were no longer together, Mercedes felt no need to cover for Monzon. She filed assault charges; he was arrested at 3 a.m. that morning in Santa Fe. When the case went to trial, Monzon ducked a six-month prison sentence by pleading "temporary insanity." Mercedes, usually quiet on the subject, said around this time, "Carlos is a great champion, but as a person he isn't the same as what the cameras show."

Two months later Monzon was arrested after assaulting a Santa Fe man named Carlos Lezcano. They'd been arguing over the price of a car when Monzon hit Lezcano in the mouth.

Then there was an incident with Oscar Bonavena. If another fighter in Argentina could rival Monzon for popularity, it was Bonavena, a perennial heavyweight contender who had even cut a rock 'n' roll single that played on Argentine radio during the 1960s. Nearly as temperamental as Monzon, he'd eventually be murdered under mysterious circumstances outside a Reno whorehouse. And in December 1974, he and Monzon almost tore each other apart.

Monzon, Bonavena, and other members of the Argentine boxing fraternity had traveled to Mexico City to watch their countryman Horacio Saldano take on Napoles. The eve of the fight saw Monzon and Bonavena get into an argument in a restaurant.

"Monzon had started mocking Bonavena during dinner," said Cherquis Bialo. "And as the dinner progressed and they emptied their glasses of white wine, the tone got worse." The gist, according to Bialo, was Monzon teasing Bonavena that his career was over, that he'd already fought the big names like Ali and Joe Frazier, and lost. Bonavena responded with an insult that hit Monzon at his core. He called Monzon ignorant, taunting him for the way he pronounced certain words. Poking fun at Monzon's intelligence, of course, was like stirring up a nest of hornets.

Even though Bonavena outweighed Monzon by forty pounds or more, Monzon "stood up and invited him to fight," said Bialo, "like teenagers in a schoolyard." Bonavena was already removing his Rolex watch when calmer heads prevailed. It was, recalled Bialo, "a highly disturbing moment. Just to be physically between them was traumatic. Bonavena was the more rational of the two. Lectoure asked me to call a cab and take Bonavena back to the hotel. The truth is that Bonavena never liked Monzon. He thought there was something negative about him. He didn't like his boxing style, or his arrogance. I think he was clearly envious. Sometimes he would denigrate Monzon in the newspapers. Monzon had never responded publicly. He had never lent himself to media controversy. That is why when they met face to face, the mutual contempt came to the surface. I was impressed that Monzon would invite a trained heavyweight boxer to fight him with bare fists, but Monzon in an alcoholic state was capable of anything."

Who would've won? It's hard to say. Both were maniacs. But with Monzon's past history of busting up saloons, it was probably good for Argentine diplomacy that no punches were thrown.

It was also good because Monzon could've been hurt. He needed to stay healthy because a promoter named Don King wanted to bring him to America.

# "He Can Be Evil"

The opponent for Monzon's U.S. debut would be Tony Licata, a young Chinese-Italian boxer out of New Orleans. The fight, part of a Madison Square Garden program created to support a closed-circuit telecast of the Muhammad Ali–Joe Bugner bout in Malaysia, was hyped as Monzon's introduction to America. Teddy Brenner, president of the Garden's boxing department, had been after Monzon for years and was alleged to have a small percentage of his contract along with Brusa, Lectoure, and others. Still, it had become increasingly difficult to lure international fighters to New York because of the state's high taxes. At the time, there were rumors that the Garden was going to abandon boxing all together. The fact that Monzon had agreed to fight there was fairly big in itself. One *Daily News* story, probably a bogus item planted by Brenner's publicity department, had the long-retired Sugar Ray Robinson calling for tickets, saying how excited he was to finally see Monzon. But when Monzon first arrived at the Garden's Hall of Fame lounge to face the press, he was met by a phalanx of cynical New York journalists. They were unimpressed. They didn't care about his gold jewelry, his cheekbones, his girlfriend, or his budding movie career.

And he didn't give a damn about them.

Monzon slouched in his chair. He gave curt answers. Without a hint of irony or humor, he proclaimed himself the greatest middleweight champion in history. When asked about some of the greats of the past, he said he'd never heard of them. His eyes flashed with anger when someone mentioned Rodrigo Valdes, but otherwise, he was as remote as a cloud. "He appeared to be bored and impatient," reported the *New York Times*. "He often glanced away as if searching for an escape."

New York reporters, some calling him the "splendid string bean of Buenos Aires," filled their columns with comments about Monzon's brusque attitude. Emile Griffith, on hand to view Monzon's introduction to New York, provided his own take on the champion. "He's an angry, nasty guy," said Griffith. "He'd spit in your eye. We are friendly now, but he can be evil."

Local sparring partners at Gleason's Gym got a dose of Monzon's evil side, complaining that he was too rough on them. Monzon, in turn, complained that New York hadn't provided him with decent sparring partners. He was moody because Susana had stayed behind in Argentina so he could focus on training. Brusa had grown concerned that Susana was distracting his fighter; she was asked to stay away until the night of the fight. This meant Monzon had nothing to do but spar and sit around in his hotel room.

At the weigh-in before the contest, Monzon and Licata were asked to pose together for a photo. Licata tried to look fierce. Monzon laughed. "Smile," Monzon said, tickling Licata under the chin. It was the only bit of personality Monzon showed that week.

The event was actually an experiment by Don King. Only a few years into his bombastic career, King felt the closed-circuit era was ending but could be saved by creating a strong live event to go along with the telecast and charging a modest admission. Other promoters had tried this, but usually with local talent, not an international name like Monzon. The idea had merit, but ticket sales were slow. As fight night arrived, King was uncharacteristically detached from the proceedings. He certainly wasn't banging the drums to make Monzon a star in New York. The reality was that King was already busy with the details of Ali's next bout, which would be in the Philippines against Joe Frazier. Monzon may have been a big deal in Argentina, but not even the blustery King could bother hyping him in the same breath as the "Thrilla in Manila."

Like many of Monzon's challengers, Licata was feisty in the early rounds but less so once Monzon began slinging punches. Monzon knocked him down in the eighth and twice more in the tenth before referee Tony Perez stopped the bout. "Let me rest for a few hours," Monzon said, "and I'll fight Valdes tomorrow."

The event drew a so-so 13,496 to the Garden, and Monzon had to share the scene with fellow Argentines Victor Galindez and Jorge Ahumada on the co-feature. Monzon had not only failed to impress the New York media, but his methodical approach to beating Licata simply wasn't dramatic enough for New York's boxing crowd. *Sports Illustrated* correspondent Mark Kram even ridiculed the Argentine mob that greeted Monzon at the consulate's postfight buffet, "attended by millionaire ranchers and others who did everything but drop palm leaves in front of Monzon as he entered." To Kram, Monzon's long reign as champion reflected only the poor quality of his opponents. "The once proud and brutally rugged middleweight division," Kram wrote, "is as arid and desolate as an atomic testing site."

Red Smith, New York's most venerated sportswriter, could barely muster any interest in Monzon, calling him a "half-champion" defending a "half-title."

◆ ◆ ◆

On December 13, 1975, an estimated six thousand fans entered the Paris Hippodrome to watch Monzon knock out French contender Gratien

Tonna at 2:02 of round five. Tonna, who took the referee's ten count while sobbing and clutching his head, claimed Monzon hit him with an illegal punch. Tonna was later fined for trying to force a disqualification. "He was crap," Monzon said.

Though promoter Sabbatini claimed the bout was a financial success, the event was a disaster. Disgusted by Tonna's nonperformance, fans grew unruly and chanted that they wanted their money back. Columnists speculated that big-time boxing in France was coming to an end.

The angst in the air seemed to fit Monzon's mood. "I'm not interested in boxing now," he said during the run-up to the fight. Physically, he was breaking down. His hands were constantly hurting, and just eight weeks earlier he'd undergone an operation on his right elbow. Also, the bout with Tonna was a major comedown in attendance compared to his previous French bouts, a sign, perhaps, that his popularity in Paris had ebbed. For that matter, Monzon wasn't even Argentina's top sports hero anymore; he'd been supplanted for the time being by Guillermo Vilas, a twenty-two-year-old tennis genius.

What hurt Monzon's popularity most at home was his divorce from Mercedes. Not only did Argentina's heavily Catholic population frown on divorces, but Susana's résumé of adult-oriented comedies assured older Argentines that Monzon had abandoned the mother of his children for a slutty clown. It didn't help that her sartorial sense ran toward pink denim.

Monzon and Susana were by now the most photographed twosome in Argentina. Journalist Alfredo Serra estimated they appeared on more than three hundred magazine covers, describing the pair as combining "the strength, beauty, fame and glamour of the world in a single couple." "It was crazy what happened to us," Susana said of the Argentine paparazzi. "They followed us everywhere, came out from under the tiles."

Susana was not just Monzon's lover. She was a mentor, the most important person he'd met since Brusa. She helped him with his reading, taught him the proper use of cutlery, and even tried to help him with his anger toward reporters. Despite his success, Monzon was still uneasy, still suspicious.

One of Monzon's recurring fears was that Susana would be ridiculed for being with a man from such a poor background. Cherquis Bialo, who had ghostwritten *My True Life*, learned personally how Monzon felt about discussing his underprivileged childhood. Monzon needed fifteen months of goading from Bialo before he'd open up about his past. He eventually talked about being born on a dirt floor, of hunting armadillos and ostriches, of the family's trek to Santa Fe, of his meager schooling, of his sisters working menial jobs so he could focus on boxing. It was quaint, and heartfelt, but after the book's initial success—three sold-out printings in less than a year—Monzon demanded it be taken out of circulation. It was never again in print. This was odd on Monzon's part, but he may have been showing classic narcissistic behavior, trying to control his image. He wanted to be known as a champion, a movie star with famous friends. He didn't want to be known as a barefoot swamp hunter.

With his twelfth title defense behind him, Monzon's future was uncertain. Rodrigo Valdes had recently earned the WBC belt by defeating Bennie Briscoe in Monte Carlo, so Monzon said he'd like to fight Valdes to get his old belt back. For a while there was talk that Monzon was being offered $650,000 to fight in Africa. Nothing came of it. Sometimes Monzon talked about retiring to his ranch with Susana, proving once and for all that their romance was not a publicity stunt.

Mostly, Monzon talked about his acting career. In the Argentine winter of 1976, he appeared in *Soñar, Soñar* ("Dream, Dream"), where he played a small-town hotel employee who quits his job to go into show business. He befriends an eccentric singer (Gian Franco Pagliaro), who leads him on a series of misadventures; the two wind up in jail, entertaining the inmates. It's an offbeat but touching movie, somewhat in the vein of *Midnight Cowboy* or *Of Mice and Men*, where two misfits come together in search of a dream. The greatest surprise was Monzon's performance. For an inexperienced actor, his work in the film was complex, full of comedy and pathos. At times he seems as vulnerable as a child. Watching him in *Soñar, Soñar,* one wonders if those closest to Monzon sometimes saw this helpless side of him, what Brusa called "the defenseless boy," and if that's why they couldn't accept his actions later in life. Watching him in this movie, you can't imagine him strangling a woman.

# One Fight/One Film

The critical acclaim for *Soñar, Soñar* had Monzon ready to hang up his gloves in favor of more movie scripts.

But there was a problem.

Movie producers only wanted Monzon if he continued fighting. He was no use to them if he retired. One movie insider put the formula to him this way: One fight would equal one film role.

Monzon didn't like the proposition, but it made sense. During the 1970s, athletes from Joe Namath to Ken Norton and even Muhammad Ali were used in movie roles as long as they were active in their sport. Though there were exceptions, most athletes found that once their sports career ended, the acting parts grew less distinguished. If they were lucky, they'd get a deal to endorse beer or joint-pain ointments. Monzon, though, actually loved movies. Sometimes he'd skip training and sneak off to a local theater to take in two features in a row. "He liked being in the movies," said Argentine journalist Carlos Irusta. "He wasn't just doing it to meet women." And as Monzon showed in *Soñar, Soñar,* he had a talent for acting, and a willingness to play against his macho image. In only his second film, he was doing everything from crying to pratfalls.

His third film, *The Last Round*, was an Italian production where Monzon played a former boxer involved with two rival Mafia families. Director Stelvio Massi, who had been a camera operator on Sergio Leone's classic spaghetti western *A Fistful of Dollars*, required Monzon do little more than look tough and have a few fight scenes. Perhaps to cash in on the success of *La Mary*, Susana was cast along with Monzon. The difference was that now he received much higher billing. *The Last Round* wasn't a big hit, but it developed a small cult following among fans of 1970s Italian action movies.

Alain Delon, who had promoted Monzon's bout with Jose Napoles, now talked of producing a film for his new friend to star in, perhaps an action vehicle for the two of them. Though the project never came off, the friendship between Delon and Manzon seemed real. Delon had done a bit of boxing in his youth and no doubt admired Monzon, and Monzon's ever-growing ego was fed by having a famous actor friend. They were a perfect yin-and-yang pairing: Monzon made Delon seem tougher, and Delon made Monzon seem more sophisticated. Delon gave Monzon advice on how to dress, how to order wine, and where to have his suits made. Between Susana and Delon, Monzon was being as carefully groomed as any young movie star.

Yet Monzon wasn't an easy fit for the movie business. He struggled to learn lines, he ignored shooting schedules to take vacations with Susana, and he sometimes forgot his own strength during fight scenes. He once slugged an Italian stuntman so hard that he sent the poor fellow to the hospital for eight stitches. And when German actor Helmut Berger made the mistake of flirting with him, Monzon threw the gay man across the room and had to be restrained.

"He was violent," said Héctor Cavallero. Susana had left him in order to be with Monzon, but Cavallero remained friendly with both of them. "His serious problem was alcohol," Cavallero said. "And it didn't take more than two drinks."

Rodolfo Sabbatini, who invested money in Monzon's film career, was amused by Monzon's hostility. After all, Monzon was no longer a rough street kid. He was a man in his thirties, wealthy enough to have recently purchased a Mercedes Benz dealership. Yet he always seemed to be boiling. With eerie foresight, Sabbatini described Monzon as "a potential killer."

Meanwhile, Brusa and Lectoure were concerned about Susana's growing influence on Monzon. They were especially unhappy with the way she lingered around his training quarters. Sometimes she even spoke for him at press conferences. Monzon's hatred of journalists had grown, so he was happy to let her do the talking. Letting her handle the press also appealed to his vision of himself as too important to bother with reporters. Eventually, Lectoure and Brusa demanded Susana stay clear of his sparring sessions and take a separate hotel room when they traveled somewhere for a fight. Monzon was angry but relented. "His love life came ahead of everything," said Lectoure.

The main reason for the concern over Susana was that Monzon had finally agreed to fight Rodrigo Valdes. "This one," said Sabbatini, promoting the bout in Monte Carlo, "will be very special. Very close. Very artistic in a violent sort of way."

With Valdes recognized as the WBC titleholder, and Monzon still holding the WBA belt, the matchup was a natural. But the idea that they were both considered champions irked Monzon.

"For me," Monzon said, "Valdes is just another challenger. So far he has only fought second-class boxers. There is only one Monzon. Valdes never had to fight a Monzon."

Despite Monzon's tough talk, his reasons for taking the fight were largely tied to his acting dreams. One fight, one movie. That was the formula.

But fighting Valdes was a hard way to get a movie deal. Valdes was a terror; he'd even knocked out Bennie Briscoe, something Monzon had failed to do in two fights. And unlike many of Monzon's opponents, he had no fear of Monzon.

"I'm going to bash in his pretty actor's face," Valdes said.

Monzon responded, "I'm going to send Valdes back to Colombia looking like he was run over by a locomotive." He added that he wanted the fight to go the full fifteen-round limit. "That way I can watch him bleed slowly until the end."

They were made for each other.

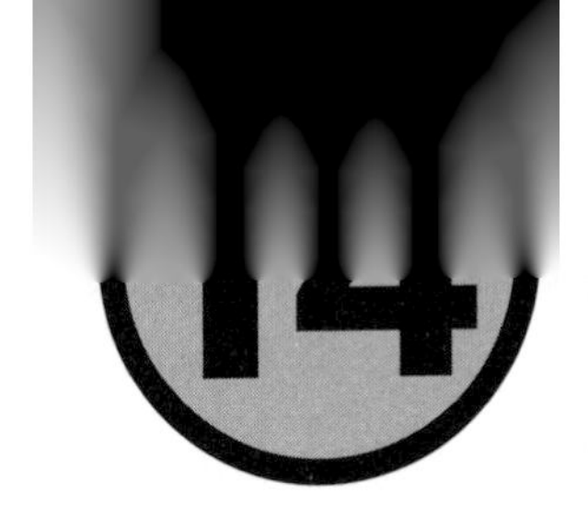

# Superstar

Monte Carlo buzzed with excitement during the week of the fight. The contest was set for June 26, 1976, at the Luis II stadium, the site of Monzon's second win over Nino Benvenuti and his second win over Emile Griffith. Monzon was at the peak of his stardom, with a grand arrival worthy of a visiting raja. "When his caravan arrived at the Hermitage Hotel," reported *Sports Illustrated*, "he spilled out in a radiant white ensemble with blonde actress Susana Gimenez, his co-star in the Argentine film *La Mary*, and forty-eight pieces of luggage in tow. Then the one-time shoeshine boy from the Pampas swept through the Belle Epoque Rotunda, where W. Somerset Maugham once took his tea, and disappeared in a swirl of handlers and photographers."

Rodrigo Valdes was also popular in Monte Carlo. With his backstory of fighting bare-knuckle in carnivals—and fighting sharks during his years as a depth-charge fisherman—Valdes was an unusual character, the polar opposite of the boxing movie star. And with Gil Clancy in his corner, who had had two close looks at Monzon during his time as Griffith's trainer, it seemed Valdes had a lot in his favor. Yet he barely made weight for the bout, stepping on the scale six times before hitting the middleweight mark. Valdes was also in mourning after learning just days earlier that his brother had been killed in a street fight.

Monzon's training hadn't been worry free, either. Along with an upcoming film shoot to think about, an old court case was hanging over his head. When the fight was over, he would return to Argentina, where a judge was ready to sentence him for hitting photographer Daniel Moreno. Monzon had injured the man's eye and was facing a possible prison sentence.

"This was a difficult time for him," said Cherquis Bialo. "He had so much on his mind; his weight, the pain in his hands, and the fact that the end of his career was approaching. He wanted to retire as the champion. He didn't want to lose in the ring. All the risk was on him, all the expectations. And things were not ideal with Susana. They were having problems."

Juan Carlos Lectoure didn't hide his concern. He was blunt, explaining to the press that Monzon was only seventy percent of what he had once been. Perhaps to drum up interest in the bout, he said previous opponents had no chance with Monzon, but now, with Monzon distracted by Susana, Valdez was actually in position to score an upset. Monzon insisted Susana was not a distraction, but an inspiration. When Monzon entered the ring on fight night, he ignored the celebrities in the front row and, according to one onlooker, stared directly at Susana, "who swiveled to ringside in a shimmer of gold lamé."

Monzon used his underrated boxing skills to control the bout, but Valdes came as advertised, a small earthquake of a fighter trying to smash his way past Monzon's guard. By the eleventh, Valdes looked exhausted, slumped in his corner between rounds, his seconds applying ice packs above each eye. Valdes and Clancy would later complain that Monzon fouled the entire fight without a single warning from the referee, but the truth is that Monzon was too slick for Valdes. In the fourteenth round, Monzon landed a sneaky right hand that put Valdes on the canvas and sent a roar rippling through the crowd. After the fifteenth, all three scorecards were for Monzon, 146-144, 147-145, and 148-144.

"It wasn't my hardest fight, not at all," Monzon said. "He hurt me once, but he was too small for Carlos Monzon."

Monzon earned $250,000, regained the WBC belt, and flew back to Argentina with Susana. They were set to star together in another Italian film.

The following months were a typical rough patch for Monzon: In July he was involved in another car accident, this time when his car hit a school bus, injuring himself and his adopted son Carlos Raul; that same month he was attacked by an unnamed person in Parana, but for one of the rare times in his life he allegedly didn't fight back; on August 3, he was sentenced to eighteen months in jail for his assault on Daniel Moreno; judge Carlos Echauri allowed an appeal, giving Monzon 120 days to go to Rome and finish a film obligation. That same month, Monzon applied for a visa to visit America but was denied because of his growing list of assault charges and legal problems. Finally, Italian actress Crippy Yocard claimed Monzon had impregnated her; he said he had never met her.

Monzon got a break in December when his sentence for hitting Moreno was "lifted" after an appeal, but shortly after that he injured his foot playing soccer with some buddies.

As the year ended, he limped into Rome to resume his acting career.

◆ ◆ ◆

Monzon spent the early part of 1977 in Italy filming *Macho Killers* (aka *El Macho*), a cheap, muddled production from schlock monger Riccardo Billi. Known for such titles as *Super Stooges versus the Wonder Women*, Billi had no higher ambition than to make quick films for a quick buck. He was also exploiting Monzon's nickname. "In Argentina," explained Alain Delon, "they don't call him 'Macho.' They call him 'El Macho.' That is the perfection of virility." Stories off the set claimed Monzon was like a child with his prop pistol, sneaking up behind cast members and shooting blanks in the air.

Upon the completion of *Macho Killers* in March, Monzon was set to fight again. Various opponents had been mentioned in the previous months, including British contender Alan Minter, American Mike Colbert, and South Africa's Elijah "Tap Tap" Makhathini. Even Bennie Briscoe's name was mentioned for a possible bout in France. Then it was announced that his next bout would be a rematch with Valdes in Monte Carlo. "No matter what the result," Monzon said, "this is my last fight. I've been fighting for more than seventeen years, and I'm tired of making the sacrifices that boxing requires."

The fight was signed for July 7, 1977, with amazing pomp and ceremony. Monzon's farewell would be promoted as a major international event. Top Rank Inc. handled the television packaging and, with more than thirty countries on the broadcast list, promised Monzon–Valdes II would be seen by more people than any previous bout not involving Ali. It was billed as the richest middleweight bout ever, with Sabbatini pushing tickets priced as high as 1,200 francs ($240), another reported record. This, fans were reminded, was the last chance to see Monzon, who was hailed in the prefight publicity as boxing's top fighter pound for pound, and possibly the greatest middleweight of all time.

What Sabbatini and Top Rank had to be concerned about was Monzon's physical condition. He'd been away from fighting for nearly a year. The closest he'd come to boxing was in choreographed fights on movie sets—that is, unless you count a skirmish with American light heavyweight Jesse Burnett in Monte Carlo that May. Burnett had flown in for a fight with Argentine Miguel Angel Cuello, and as a favor to Sabbatini, Monzon agreed to an impromptu photo shoot with Burnett in a hotel lobby. Characteristic of Monzon, he started insulting Burnett. This led to a scuffle that, according to British columnist John Rodda, "ended with Monzon on the floor." Most reports have the fight broken up before it got out of hand. Strangely, after the melee, Monzon put his arm around Burnett and the two smiled for the cameras.

The fiasco in the foyer aside, Monzon was coming off his longest inactive stretch since he'd started boxing. Expectedly, he looked terrible in the early days of training. He'd set up camp in Rome in mid-June but was showing the classic signs of an aging fighter. He was lackluster. He tended to recline on the ropes and spar in a lazy, pawing manner. An American sparring partner, Willie Warren, told the AP that Monzon had been awful during that first week in Rome, "so slow my ten-year-old kid could've zapped him." Bored with traditional training, Monzon was content to wrap himself in heavy clothes to sweat his way down to his fighting weight.

Monzon was in such miserable shape that he wouldn't even train in a gym. Instead, a small ring was set up in a private room at his hotel, purportedly so he could spar without fans interrupting, but mostly to keep reporters from seeing his rusty condition. During an early sparring session with local amateur Mario Caputo, Monzon walked into a punch that sliced open his left eyebrow. Worse than any cut he'd ever suffered in an actual contest, it caused the Valdes fight to be postponed until July 30.

While letting the cut heal, Monzon announced a plan to grant rematches to Valdes, Briscoe, and Licata. But as July 30 approached, he changed his tone. Valdes, he said, would be his last opponent, "and I will go out flaming. I will give everyone a knockout that boxing will not forget."

Monzon knew he had only one fight left in him.

He'd barely win it.

# El Macho's Last Ride

The rematch with Valdes started out as a replay of their first bout. It was at the same Monte Carlo stadium, with such international movie stars as Jean-Paul Belmondo, Omar Sharif, and Gerard Depardieu in the audience. As he'd done thirteen months earlier, Monzon was boxing and moving, toying with his shorter opponent. Then, near the end of the second round, Valdes found an opening. Slashing through the jungle of Monzon's long arms, he landed an overhand right flush on Monzon's chin. Monzon fell to his knees.

It had been years since anyone knocked him down, not since the early days of his career. Monzon was up quickly, raising his arms high to show he was unhurt, but by the end of the round he was bleeding from a gash on the side of his nose. Gil Clancy had promised that Valdes would be much better this time; the Colombian wasn't distracted by a family tragedy, as he had been in their first fight.

Though Sabbatini and Brusa claimed Monzon had trained hard, there'd been concern that the champion was past his prime. He'd only agreed to fight Valdes again when he was promised $500,000—at the time the highest payday ever for a middleweight champion—plus another $60,000 for Argentine TV rights. Still, Sabbatini praised Monzon, saying he was in "superb condition. It just proves to me that he is an animal. A beautiful animal."

But in the days before the fight, Monzon appeared tense. "It was like the fight was a huge burden," said Cherquis Bialo. Monzon's hand ached. He was short with journalists. He yelled at photographers, threatening to break their cameras. He began complaining that he felt ill, and sought out a doctor for vitamin shots to boost his energy. At the last moment he had Susana flown in from Argentina. "If she doesn't come, I won't fight," Monzon said, daring anyone to confront him on the subject.

At one point Monzon barged into a Monte Carlo gift shop where Bialo and another writer were standing. He began yelling. With a sweep of his arm, Monzon smashed a display of expensive perfumes, sending shards of glass all across the store. Then he pointed to Bialo and said, "After I beat Valdes I'm coming to your room to break your face. I'll kill you!"

Bialo wasn't sure why he had drawn Monzon's wrath, but he quickly moved his typewriter and luggage into another writer's room.

Adding to Monzon's mental stress was an incident that took place just moments before the bout, when a group of rowdy fans began heckling Susana at ringside, singing obscene songs and mocking her. Alain Delon and three bodyguards invaded the group's section and started swinging. When word of the ringside melee reached Monzon, he began to worry. Would Susana be safe during the fight? It was too much to have on his mind as he prepared to face Valdes, but the knockdown in round two seemed to alert him to the job at hand.

Monzon used his jab to control rounds three, four, and five, but in the sixth Valdes took the fight back, hammering Monzon's body and head with short, jolting punches. The momentum changed again in the tenth when Monzon began firing his right hand. One of Monzon's punches was so hard it knocked Valdes tottering halfway across the ring. The next two rounds were also Monzon's. He ripped open gashes in the Colombian's face, punching until his yellow gloves were stained the color of undercooked meat.

Prior to round thirteen, Monzon told Brusa that his right hand was done. The old war club that had served him for so many years felt dead inside his glove. "I don't know if I can use it anymore," Monzon said. Brusa told him that Valdes was tired and could probably be beaten with one hand. But as Monzon spent the next round jabbing with his left, Valdes found a new burst of energy and scratched his way back into the fight. As damaged as his right hand was, and as much as it pained him to do so, Monzon had no choice but to use it in the fourteenth. This was the hand that had made him a champion, and now it was as fragile as an ancient piece of wood. Yet he threw it, and threw it some more, directly into Valdes's swollen face. The blows weren't enough to stop the challenger, but they were enough to slow him down.

The fifteenth, which turned out to be the final round of Monzon's career, was perhaps the most grueling three minutes he'd ever endured. Valdes, his face distorted by lumps, his mouth pouring blood, his eyes nearly banged shut, kept tramping forward, shooting out tired flurries. Monzon, his face gray with exhaustion, his thin legs barely able to keep him vertical, mauled with his left and slapped with his nearly useless right. On this night he wasn't a bully. He wasn't a front-runner. Officials didn't protect him. He was a fighter, as brave and competitive as any who had come before him. "In the last round," reported *Sports Illustrated*, "they reduced boxing to its most primitive form."

After the round ended, as the audience of ten thousand bellowed its approval, Monzon walked unsteadily to his corner and collapsed onto his stool. He was smiling a bit and seemed satisfied with his performance, but when he stood up to listen to the scores, he was so tired that he had to lean on his cornermen. The scorecards went his way: 144-141, 147-144, and 145-143. Though Valdes felt certain he had won, most agreed that Monzon had done enough to retain his title for the fourteenth time. He'd shown his age, but he'd done enough.

Monzon dedicated the fight to Argentina, gave Lectoure a hug, and then announced his retirement in the ring.

"I think I showed everyone I'm one of the great ones," Monzon said. "But it's over now. For sure. I'm going to start living like a human being tonight."

In his dressing room, Monzon was the picture of an utterly spent human being. His young son Abel hugged him and said that he'd cried when Valdes knocked him down. There was a tender moment between father and son, with Monzon telling Abel that men are often knocked down in life but they have to get back up. Then Monzon stretched out on the rubbing table. He let out a short laugh, a release of pressure after such a hard contest or a sigh of disbelief that his career was over.

It had been his one hundredth recorded fight, though he often said there'd been another sixteen or so that went unrecorded. His official record was astonishing, 87-3-9, with fifty-nine of his wins coming by knockout. The no-contest early in his career put him at an even one hundred fights. He'd put up one of the best ledgers of boxing's modern era, with a thirteen-year unbeaten streak of seventy-nine bouts.

He had done it with arthritis, a growing reliance on alcohol, and enough personal problems to give most men an ulcer. He'd done it while dealing with the police, and avoiding prison. And he did it all across Argentina. He'd fought not just in Buenos Aires and Santa Fe, but all over the country. He fought in small, densely packed cities and in underdeveloped areas where sugar farmers and mill workers spent their hard-earned money to see him. His fourteen successful title defenses set a record for the weight class that would stand until Bernard Hopkins surpassed it in 2002. He earned more money than previous middleweight champions, and drew enormous crowds in Argentina and France. Though Monzon never cracked the American market, in the final two years of his title reign, he was being hailed in America as an all-time great.

Monzon lay silently on the rubbing table and didn't move. He was a portrait in still life, a champion in repose after his final victory. His handlers tore off the wrapping from his aching hands, removed his boots, as if stripping a warrior of his armor. He lay still, as if the pain of one hundred bouts had finally caught up to him. He was nearly thirty-five—old for a fighter in 1977—and had been fighting top opposition for seven years. He'd heard cheers and jeers; he'd had garbage thrown at him; he'd gone as far as his right hand could take him.

He threw a gala dinner at his hotel on Sunday, with one hundred and fifty guests. Those close to him wondered if his retirement would stick. Sabbatini doubted Monzon could stay away from boxing. "He needs it," Sabbatini said, "because he is an animal and he lives for macho."

On August 30, 1977, Monzon officially announced his retirement at a banquet in Buenos Aires. As was customary, he'd contacted the WBA and WBC to say he was no longer fighting and would relinquish his title belts for others to fight over. At the end of the evening, Monzon addressed the three hundred or so actors, singers, sportscasters, and journalists who had come to pay tribute to him.

"This is a very hard thing for me to do," Monzon said. "Always, when a boxer is starting out, it takes a lot of work to make it to the top. And then, tonight, it was such a quick thing. I sent the telegrams in less than twenty minutes. I am no longer the champion."

There would be occasional rumors of a comeback, but Monzon stayed retired. In public he'd said that the second Valdes bout had been difficult because he'd been living the playboy lifestyle, but he knew the truth: At thirty-five, it was time to quit. Valdes had taken him too close to the edge.

◆ ◆ ◆

In the aftermath of the Monte Carlo bout, Susana appeared in public wearing sunglasses to cover a swollen eye. She claimed she'd stumbled in her hotel room, but a story surfaced years later that she had actually sought the help of sportswriter Alfredo Serra, asking if she could hide in his room rather than face the fury of Monzon. Serra wrote of her frenzied dash down the corridor, "A beautiful whirlwind dressed only in a long nightgown. It was the unmistakable Susana Gimenez, shouting: 'Alfie, defend me from this monster that wants to kill me!'"

Despite Serra's account, Susana insisted that no violence had taken place in Monte Carlo. Reporters, she said, were always looking for blood where there was none. Still, she left Monzon shortly after he retired from boxing. "He changed if he drank alcohol," Susana said. "He was an alcoholic, nothing more. Nothing less."

As Susana described it, there was no drama when she left him. She simply told Monzon she was leaving. That he didn't explode when she ended their relationship is one of the mysteries of Monzon. She claimed it was an easy split, that she simply worked up some courage and told him that enough was enough. "Carlos didn't take it very well," she said, "but he had to accept it."

It's possible that Monzon thought he had gotten all he could out of the relationship. In a short time, he'd actually become a bigger star than Susana, getting higher billing in *The Last Round* and *Macho Killers*. Having surpassed her in that regard, he may have felt she was of no more use to him. It's also likely that he had one or two other women ready to take her place. It is also possible that Susana was such an independent woman that he was actually resigned to letting her go her own way. "He wanted to control her," said Bialo. "But he couldn't control her."

Susana never depicted Monzon as an abuser. Witnesses and friends said otherwise. One said Monzon once broke a framed picture over Susana's head, and another claimed Susana sometimes appeared for movie work covered in bruises that had to be camouflaged by makeup artists. But she insisted he'd only struck her one time, in Naples, during the making of *The Last Round*. He'd been jealous that another actor had been friendly to her. According to Susana, Monzon's violence wasn't the cause of their breakup. She left simply because he had changed. He spent his time drinking and playing cards with his friends. "He stopped fighting and had nothing to do during the day," she said. "That was his problem."

Though she downplayed his violent nature, she occasionally let it slip that Monzon was a bad man. She told one interviewer years later, "I had to get out of there or I was going to end up like Alicia."

# Desperate Sundown

A strange thing happened to Monzon in retirement: He became a better fighter.

The boxer who had often been dismissed as a classless thug was now revered as an all-time great. In 1983, *The Ring* magazine said that had Monzon been American, he "would've been more popular than Muhammad Ali." Budd Schulberg, noted author and longtime boxing observer, considered Monzon part of a "golden circle of middleweight immortals," and placed him on a short list of eight "genius fighters" that included Ali, Sugar Ray Robinson, Roberto Duran, Archie Moore, Willie Pep, Joe Louis, and Henry Armstrong.

During the next decade, when lists were made of the top middleweights, or of great championship reigns, Monzon's name would always be near the top. In 1982 it was reported that the camp of reigning middleweight champion Marvelous Marvin Hagler made an offer to Monzon, hoping the now forty-year-old might consider coming out of retirement. Monzon smirked. Hagler, he said, "couldn't beat me with a stick." Then, with the old cockiness, Monzon added, "I fought a lot of Haglers. But he never fought a Monzon."

In June of 1990, with the establishment of the International Boxing Hall of Fame in Canastota, New York, Monzon would be part of the first group of inductees, voted in alongside such iconic stars as Ali, Robinson, and Louis. Not bad for a fighter who spent a few fights dodging rotten fruit.

But as Monzon's reputation as a boxer grew, his dreams of movie stardom evaporated. As expected, once his boxing career was over, his acting roles diminished.

As the 1970s came to an end, Monzon published a memoir in France. Perhaps translators embellished his thoughts, but this new book was drastically different in tone from *My True Life*. In *Moi, Carlos Monzon*, where he'd once romanticized San Javier, now he described it as a monotonous landscape with "the stale odor of putrefaction." He dismissed his neighbors as "peons with pitiful incomes," and his own family household as "twelve children crying famine and their parents helpless to help them." He railed at his father's "paltry salary" and the lack of education that had afflicted the Monzons for several generations. The new neighborhood in the capital was no better than San Javier, a "shantytown," he called it, describing Santa Fe as "a city of pariahs."

He was sly enough to publish it in France, not Argentina.

A seasoned narcissist determined to place himself above all others, Monzon insisted on being viewed as a rich celebrity. In many of his post-career interviews, he bragged about his successes, his movie roles, and his business ventures. He also ridiculed other fighters for staying in boxing too long. They could continue fighting forever and get their heads banged in, but not Monzon.

In reality, Monzon was floundering. He piled up one bad business deal after another. He blew large investments on everything from imported Korean television sets, to a clothing store, to a perfume factory. He was linked to more actresses, but none stayed with him for long. There were also more legal problems, including a twenty-eight-day stint in a Santa Fe jail for illegal possession of a gun, at least one barroom brawl, a lawsuit from a man claiming Monzon beat him up in a Santa Fe bowling alley, and a near tragedy when Monzon smashed his Mercedes Benz into a bus and injured three people. If Monzon had hit unimaginable heights during his career, in retirement he was just another hopeless ex-pug. He gained weight and upped his cigarette intake to two packs a day.

He also met Alicia Muniz. Things were good for a time.

# Alicia

"I, Alba Alicia Muniz Calatayud lived with Mr. Carlos Monzon from May 1979 to August 12, 1986."

Thus began a civil lawsuit filed by Alicia after their third separation. She described how Monzon was always drunk and aggressive, and how he "went crazy" on August 11, 1986, saying he would break everything she owned and "then he was going to kill me."

He had even slapped her in front of their son, Maxi.

She left him, returned, and left him again in 1987. He was, she said, out of control.

Alicia had been a model before they met, and a belly dancer, and had allegedly appeared uncredited in some movies. She was also managing a popular hair salon. That she was successful at just about everything she tried tells us a lot about her. She was a bright woman, resourceful, with personality. She didn't have the burning ambitions of Susana Gimenez, but she was sunny and lively. She met Monzon through mutual friends. The story of how they met varies depending on who tells it. It was either on a plane ride, in an airport, or in a cafe in Rio de Janeiro.

A year passed between their first meeting and when Monzon spotted Alicia in a restaurant. He didn't even recognize her as the woman he'd met before; he simply asked a waiter to introduce them. When Alicia explained that they'd met the previous year, Monzon turned on the charm. He began appearing at the salon where she worked, as if courting the entire staff. He won her over. They sneaked off to Miami to wed because Argentine law didn't recognize his divorce from Mercedes. Once married, she put her ambitions aside and devoted herself to him.

"I made concessions because I loved him," Alicia once said. She described herself as a kind of life preserver for Monzon, who was feeling old. "I was the vitality injection he needed. I was that piece of youth that tied him to life. Why did he choose me? I don't know. I tried being a Samaritan. I think I helped him."

But Monzon was unpredictable. He abused Alicia both verbally and physically. She had packed her suitcase many times during their first two years together, ready to leave. He'd always charm her into staying. The birth of Maxi on December 28, 1981, seemed to calm Monzon for a while. He made grand pronouncements to the press that he was looking forward to settling down with his new little family. But Monzon's new leaf was all a big, meaningless show. By 1983 Alicia had moved out for the first time. She told reporters that Monzon was drinking too much. There'd been a loud argument in a nightclub where witnesses heard Alicia say she was tired of being hit.

"It is terrible," Alicia said of Monzon's behavior. "The emotional ups and downs, the instability. Feeling loved and protected, and suddenly experiencing the opposite. One gets worn out." Alicia once described Monzon to a journalist as a man who was afraid of losing his maleness, a man who couldn't be left alone.

As their marriage collapsed, Alicia returned to modeling. She needed money for Maxi's care, but Monzon wouldn't help. He wanted to control Alicia financially, hoping to manipulate her into coming back to him.

The idea that Alicia would survive without him agitated Monzon. He told her that he didn't like to see her working, that it made him look bad. She ignored him. One of Alicia's friends from modeling, Beba Lorena, told *Gente* magazine that Monzon was constantly harassing Alicia on the phone, sometimes as often as three calls per day. "He would even harass me," Lorena said, "asking me how much money Alicia was making." He sent threatening messages to Alicia's friends, including photographers, other models, hair stylists, anybody involved in her new career. Lorena also offered her own theory about Alicia's ill-fated visit to Mar del Plata: "We had a job in Punta del Esta, but she went to Mar del Plata first, to show him how pretty she was after recently slimming down for modeling. Oh my God, why?"

Actor Facha Martel's son Roman recalled the Monzon of this period as a gruff character who talked often about violence. In 2019 Roman told *La Nacion*, "I never liked Monzon. I thought he was gross. He gave me a huge knife and told me, 'If you ever have problems with a policeman, just dig this all the way in.'" Asked if he'd ever witnessed Monzon being violent with Alicia, the son of El Facha said, "No, but he was half a beast." Even at age nine, Roman could sense something was wrong between Monzon and Alicia. "He always seemed quite rough to me," Roman said, "and she was a sweet, very divine girl."

In 1986 Monzon got a rare television gig, appearing in *Supermingo*, a short-lived comedy show that starred Juan Carlos Altavista as a tramp character named "Mingo." Monzon seemed to have fun with his cameo. As the final credits rolled, he put his arm around the show's star, sniggering over some inside joke.

But in roughly the same time period as he was laughing with Mingo, Alicia was telling police that Monzon was a madman who wanted to kill her. The Villa Urquiza police station in Buenos Aires had a stack of complaints against Monzon from Alicia and her mother. The complaints, which were made in 1986 and 1987 and even included photos of her bruises, were kept from the public until years after Alicia's death.

◆ ◆ ◆

Their final hours together:

They were at the Provincial Hotel in Mar del Plata with two friends, Velasco Ferrero and Maria Eugenia Zorzenon. They were on the first floor of the hotel, which was a small casino. Monzon and Alicia sat apart. As Zorzenon recalled, the pair seemed cold to each other. They didn't kiss. They didn't hold hands. They didn't speak.

Monzon spent the evening drinking champagne—the table of four reportedly went through seven bottles of Baron B—and losing money at roulette. He'd spin the wheel, lose, come back to the table, sulk, drink more, and then try his luck again. He drank a lot, but to Zorzenon he didn't seem particularly drunk. He was just quiet. Brooding.

Alicia looked beautiful in what Zorzenon called "a Hindu dress," but appeared to be bored. At one point she began speaking loudly to Zorzenon, saying she planned to get married again someday, but not to Monzon. Zorzenon couldn't tell if Alicia was joking, or drunk, or trying to goad Monzon. "Be careful," Zorzenon said. "He'll knock your teeth out."

Facha Martel showed up later in the evening with a young woman at his side. He invited Alicia and Monzon to an event at Club Penarol. That was the last Zorzenon saw of them. "I was sure they were going to fight later," she said. "It was obvious."

Investigative journalist Jorge Joury canvassed the neighborhood where Alicia died. A witness claimed that a taxi pulled up to 1567 Pedro Zanni Street at dawn. Monzon dragged Alicia out of the car and attacked her right on the sidewalk. According to the witness, Monzon "had her by the hair and hit her relentlessly." Medical examiners would determine that Alicia had been struck at least twice by what were deemed "hard" punches. Alicia was described by the witness as crouching down to avoid Monzon's slaps, but he apparently hit her hard enough to draw blood. It was determined by investigators that Alicia's blood "ran the entire perimeter of the house."

This contradicted Monzon's own story that they didn't start fighting until they were inside.

He'd been hitting her long before that.

◆ ◆ ◆

Facha Martel woke Maxi that morning.

As Martel guided him out through a side door, Maxi wanted to know why so many police cars were parked outside.

Martel thought fast. He explained that the police were there for a movie.

Maxie wanted to know if his mom and dad were in the movie.

Yes, Martel said.

From there, Martel took Maxi to the home of another friend. Many hours later, the boy was taken to a nearby pizzeria. Maxi was surprised to see his grandfather there, sitting by himself at a table. This was Alicia's father, Hector, who had already been to the morgue to identify his daughter's body. Now he had the task of explaining to Maxi that the police hadn't been there for a movie after all.

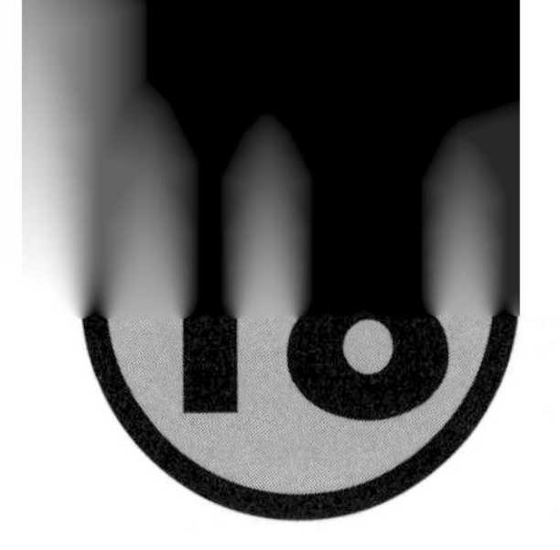

# The Lady on the Bricks

The crime seemed ahead of its time. The washed-up celebrity, the scandal, the attractive woman dead in her underwear; it should've happened in California years later in between the deeds of those tabloid champions, O. J. Simpson and Robert Blake.

The victim was beautiful, even in death, even with her body nearly broken in two. The suspect was tall, powerful. Calm.

In a 2013 interview, prosecutor Carlos Pelliza was asked about Monzon's behavior in their first meetings after his arrest. In the manner of the unfeeling psychopath, Monzon showed no remorse, no accountability. "He was not too worried about what had happened," Pelliza said.

In America, the reaction was blasé. Outside of pulpy fight magazines going on about a supposed "middleweight curse," Monzon wasn't going to make many headlines in America. "Why," asked a *Washington Post* columnist, "at a moment of great national crisis, were Argentines so wrapped up in this police-blotter soap opera?" Put plainly, this was Argentina's story. Monzon was Argentina's Elvis, Babe Ruth, and Ali, all rolled into one sneering package. Film crews and journalists descended upon Pedro Zanni Street like military invaders.

Meanwhile, Argentine columnists were divided on how to discuss Monzon. "Argentines have done badly in indulging Carlos Monzon," wrote social commentator Bernardo Neustadt. "We are a macho society that idolizes a man who beats or violates a woman, a macho society that taught Monzon to dress up, to speak a bit better, but didn't teach him to think, a macho society that wasn't horrified when Monzon said he beat all his women. . . ." *La Nacion* declared that Argentina suffered from "an overdose of machismo" and a "grave mutation of values" that condoned men such as Monzon. Even Cherquis Bialo, who happily pissed in a cup so Monzon could pass a drug test, felt some culpability. "Journalists must assume our share of responsibility and guilt," wrote Bialo. "When we perceived and saw Monzon's behavior . . . we said nothing because the idol could not be touched."

But for every editorial that thrashed Monzon, many more suggested it was unfair to hold him accountable for his violent acts. After all, he was an uneducated man who earned a living with his fists. Monzon's twenty-three-year-old son from his first marriage, Abel, complained that the media was smearing his father. "Our papa," Abel said, "is not a murderer."

Ultimately, the Monzon story became less an opportunity for sociological debate than a morbid peep show, a chance to show lurid photos of Alicia smashed on the bricks, her bare legs still beautiful even as the life flooded out of her. It was a big nasty dollop of Mar del Plata decadence, overflowing with surface glitter and cheap celebrity. Sometimes the press changed direction and focused on Maxi. Psychologists debated in print on how the now-motherless little boy should be handled. Maxi purportedly said, "I know mommy is in heaven, but where's daddy?" The quote was gold, but had he really said it? Or was it the work of a creative journalist?

As he sat in jail awaiting his trial, Monzon blamed his situation on the jackals of the Argentine tabloids. "As soon as I get out of here I am going to live in Paris," he said, "where I have good friends and the public still remembers me well."

The press injected Susana Gimenez's name into every story, because she was now a bigger star than ever, appearing in her own TV show, *Hola Susana*.

"The whole country was following the trial," Susana said. "I read a little, I didn't see it. I didn't go either, because it didn't make sense to go."

Monzon's initial testimony was an incoherent scramble. He said he and Alicia had made love that day, as if such an erotic event would preclude a murder. Then they went out for the evening. Monzon couldn't remember much, just that he drank a lot. He and Alicia fought about money. He said Alicia had attacked him, burned him with a cigarette. He admitted to slapping her, and maybe squeezing her neck. But he couldn't explain why she'd run to the balcony. "Maybe," Monzon said, "she was afraid I was going to shoot her."

The trial was predictably sensationalistic, broadcast live for five days by radio stations across Argentina. It was a legal circus from the start, beginning with Monzon's attorney, Horacio D'Angelo, who claimed his client suffered from something called "Maxwell's amnesia." This was, D'Angelo said, "a phenomenon that arises within a few hours of an incident and produces oblivion similar to that of someone who does not remember a dream."

Adding to the almost burlesque atmosphere were the characters serving as witnesses. One man, Alfredo Arturo Moyano, swore that he saw Monzon and Alicia sitting on the railing when both went over. Moyano was easy to discredit. He didn't even live in the area.

Then there was Rafael Crisanto Baez, a local scrap collector who prowled Pedro Zanni Street most mornings. From a vantage point on the street, Baez said he could see into the window of the second floor as the murder played out. "I wanted to scream," Baez said, "but I couldn't." He claimed to witness Monzon strangle Alicia, then throw her limp body off the balcony. Baez included some unique details, such as Monzon wearing regular pants when he throttled Alicia, and then changing into pajama pants for his own jump from the balcony. Baez's testimony was colorful

("Monzon stomped her like a cat!") and would be quoted, and misquoted, for several years. He could spin a story, though. When Alicia's body landed, he said, it sounded like glass breaking.

Though Monzon's defense felt Baez was only repeating what had already appeared in newspapers, the trial turned Baez into a minor celebrity. He appeared on television shows, signed autographs, and would grant interviews for a fee. Despite coming across as an attention-starved crackpot, Baez still has supporters who believe he was integral to the trial. "He was an alcoholic," said prosecutor Pelliza, "and he suffered from media pressure. To satisfy his interlocutors, he said things that had not happened. But at the police station and before the judge, at the beginning, he had impeccable testimony."

Stranger still was the situation with the cab driver. A fellow named Pedro Tonini testified that he had dropped Monzon and Alicia off at Martel's, and that the two had seemed happy together. Yet during the trial it was revealed that Tonini hadn't been the driver. The real driver had been intimidated by Monzon's friends, and Tonini had been paid to testify by Monzon's defense team.

Eventually, the forensic findings of Dr. Jorge Tonelli were more damning than any of the testimonies. Alicia's injuries were simply not consistent with someone who had fallen from a balcony. There were no wrist fractures, as there would've been if she'd been conscious and tried to break her fall. She had to have been unconscious, or dead, and the damage to her face and throat showed that she'd been beaten and strangled. Still, the defense argued there wasn't enough evidence to convict Monzon of murder. "There are only guesses," D'Angelo said.

The prosecution's final statement was highly dramatic, describing how Monzon threw Alicia from the balcony "with all his might, causing her to break her skull."

Monzon spoke briefly on his own behalf. "I am innocent," he said. He talked about how he missed Maxi and still loved Alicia, adding, "I believe in justice."

But Monzon's sense of justice was skewed. Judge Alicia Ramos Fondeville would recount years later that the defense team tried to intimidate her with tactics more suited to the trial of a Mob boss. "I was very afraid," she said. "I was threatened." The judge claimed Monzon had even hired "barra bravas," the Argentine equivalent of soccer hooligans, to stalk her. But Fondeville held firm during the trial, at one point yelling, "Tell the truth, Monzon!"

On July 3, 1989, the three-judge panel found Monzon guilty of murder and sentenced him to eleven years in prison, time he could reduce with good behavior. He was also ordered to pay $5,000 in compensation to Alicia's father. Years later, Judge Fondeville said the trial was groundbreaking, if only because of Monzon's celebrity status. "I have heard since then that people think it was a light sentence," Fondeville said, "but at the time people were surprised that such a famous person was going to prison at all. Rich people did not go to prison." The court's official statement about Monzon was, "He did not kill coldly; he was influenced by circumstances . . . but he acted with full awareness of the criminality of his acts."

Monzon listened to the verdict without any visible emotion. He was overheard telling his children, "This isn't over yet. We have to fight it."

After the verdict, a mob of Monzon's supporters chased the Muniz family lawyer for a hundred yards before police officers broke up the chase and escorted the lawyer to safety.

Meanwhile, a reporter asked Monzon what he would yell to the heavens if he had a chance.

Monzon said he would scream that he didn't do it.

◆ ◆ ◆

He found himself at the Batán prison, alone in a cell. He chain-smoked Marlboros and read the Bible. He appreciated the irony. He'd spent many years in luxury hotels with a Bible on the nightstand, but it wasn't until he was in a dirty prison that he picked one up. He read it. He liked it. He had conversations with God in his head. He told a reporter that God visited him in his cell. According to Monzon, God was a kind man with a long white beard and green eyes.

Brusa visited him in prison, accompanied by some reporters. "I have faith in you," Brusa said. Monzon sat before his old trainer and quietly wept.

The ubiquitous Cherquis Bialo was assigned to write a story about the imprisoned ex-champion for *El Grafico*. The magazine that had once done full-page photo spreads of Monzon as if he were a model now wanted a tale of the ex-champion behind prison bars. Bialo was granted a visit and described Monzon looking "scared, sad, and worried." Monzon said he wanted to be dead, because death was preferable to the confinement of his cell or the humiliation of being called a killer. He claimed television journalists had orchestrated the crowds to chant "murderer" in order to get good coverage for the nightly news. "That's what makes me sick," Monzon said. "When I remember those moments I go crazy."

He told Bialo that he still loved Alicia and always would.

He said Alicia once visited him in his cell. She stood before him, telling him not to worry, that he would be out of prison soon.

Welterweight champion Jose Napoles was no match for Monzon. *El Grafico/ Getty Images*

Monzon at dinner with Susana in Buenos Aires.
*El Grafico/Getty Images*

In his American debut, Monzon scored a tenth-round TKO over Tony Licata at Madison Square Garden. *Bettman/Getty Images*

Monzon on the party circuit in France.
*Gamma-Rapho/Getty Images*

Monzon with Alicia Muniz and Jean-Claude Bouttier at the Deauville American Film Festival in France in 1983. *Gamma-Rapho/Getty Images*

Alicia lies dead at 1567 Pedro Zanni Street
in Mar del Plata. *El Grafico/Getty Images*

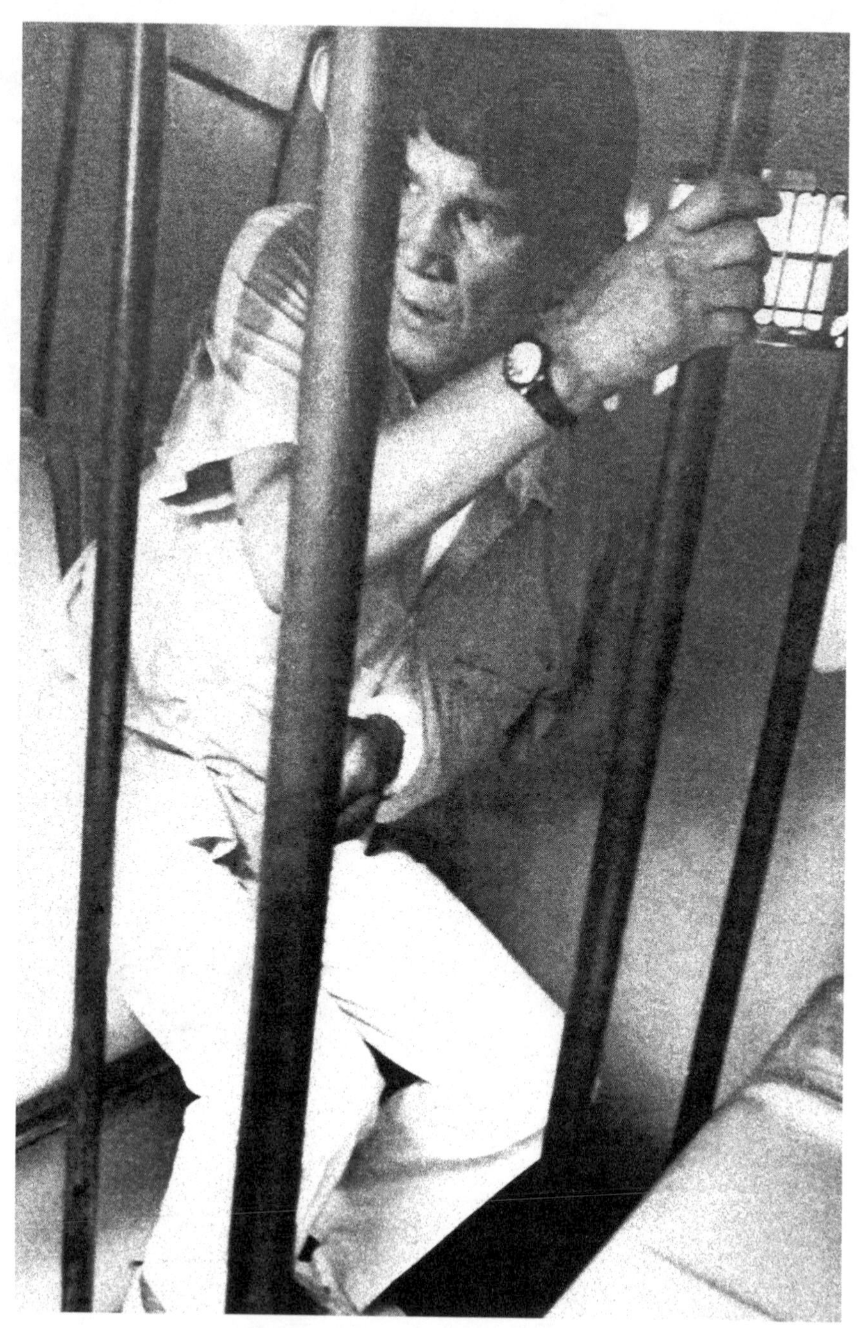

Monzon after his arrest on February 23, 1988. Notice his damaged right hand, which had been injected with novocaine throughout his career. *AP Photo*

Monzon gets the news that he's been convicted of homicide at the Criminal Appeals Court in Mar del Plata on July 3, 1989. *AP Photo*

A crowd raises the coffin of Carlos Monzon
before his burial on January 9, 1995, in Santa Fe.
*El Grafico/Getty Images*

# Murder in Mar del Plata

Here's what probably happened.

Monzon hated his life. He was living in a crowded tourist area, surrounded by second-rate actors and cokeheads. He hadn't had a real acting job in four years. He'd go to show-business parties, hoping to make some connections that could lead to an acting role, but after a while the partying became more important than the acting. Cocaine haunted every corner of the neighborhood like a malicious spirit. Monzon had become a loser. He feared others would see him that way. For the mighty Monzon, the thought of being seen as a loser was a nightmare.

He developed a dimly lit fantasy that Alicia could lift him out of the muck. When Alicia came to Mar del Plata for the weekend, he thought he had her. But she didn't come to Mar del Plata merely to spend the weekend or rekindle old feelings. She would tell him that she planned to continue with her modeling work, and reminded him that he was late with his monthly payments for Maxi.

They returned from their night out, a night where they'd been unfriendly to each other, and a witness had seen Monzon hitting Alicia.

At some point before 6 a.m., she said something that made the dynamite in his head go off.

Maybe she explained that she wasn't coming back to him, made him realize he was never getting out of this pitiful life he'd created for himself, made him realize the glorious image he'd created now meant nothing. His boxing career, his movie roles, his wardrobe, his collection of cars, his famous friends meant nothing. He was just an angry, illiterate man consumed by petty jealousies and the shame of his poor background. And he was about to be abandoned.

Monzon wasn't used to being refused. He'd always been able to charm Alicia into coming back to him. When that hadn't worked, he could bully her. Now she was standing up to him.

He had to show her he was still in charge.

Medical examiners estimated thirty-five pounds of pressure or more had been applied to Alicia's throat. Strangling only requires eleven pounds. They estimated it had been done with a two-fingered grip, probably thumb and forefinger in a kind of one-handed death clamp. It takes only twenty seconds or so to strangle someone into unconsciousness. The damage to Alicia's throat would take much longer. It wasn't done by accident or in the heat of the moment. It took a few minutes of full-on rage. Alicia had been strangled long after she had passed out. It's also rare that a strangling victim has visible marks on the neck or throat. The imprints on Alicia were clear and deep, as if someone had tried to squeeze her head off at the neck.

It has also been alleged from Baez's testimony that Monzon had actually lifted Alicia in the air as he strangled her, her feet dangling several inches off the ground.

Alicia fell to the floor, probably dead. Monzon tried to cover his ass. He took her dress, which was bloody, and disposed of it. That's why she was found nearly naked.

He took her into the bathroom and threw water on her, trying to revive her or wash off blood.

He dumped her body over the balcony to make it look like she'd fallen.

He jumped down, too, to make it appear they'd both gone over. Maybe Martel suggested it. In Monzon's state, anything Martel said would've seemed like a good idea. Monzon leaped down, but his injuries were minor; he'd broken his fall partly by landing on Alicia's corpse. Then he wandered around the house, saying there'd been an accident.

Monzon probably thought he'd get away with what he'd done because he lived in a world in which celebrities could rule countries, in which political leaders survived scandals, in which jolly TV comics lived secret lives as drug addicts, where an ignorant boxer could mix with the rich and famous, where wife beating was barely acknowledged, where the country's ongoing political strife left no time for a women's movement, where the courts didn't even have a name for the crime of a man killing a woman. It wasn't a sweet-smelling world, but it was the world Monzon lived in.

And for a long time, he had ruled a small corner of it.

The problem with Monzon was that behind the guise of this strutting peacock was an immature, self-doubting man who feared people could see through his façade. His legendary arrogance, credited by boxing experts as one of the keys to his ring successes, was the way he compensated for his fears. As a boxer, he had the perfect platform on which to prop his delicate ego. That he'd wanted to go directly from boxing to acting was probably to fulfill his excessive need for admiration. But with his boxing career over and his movie career stagnant, he had nothing to feed his ego. He was alone with his insecurities.

Did Alicia call him stupid just before he strangled her?

Did she laugh at him?

Monzon probably thought Alicia would be forever in awe of him. She wasn't. That's why she went over the balcony.

◆ ◆ ◆

There were questions about the case.

There'd been two autopsies, but the injuries to Alicia's throat weren't reported at first. The body had already been taken to Buenos Aires and buried in the Chacarita Cemetery when the court demanded it be exhumed for a second autopsy. When the lab announced Alicia's hyoid bone was broken—a sign of strangulation—Monzon's camp accused the examiners of damaging the bone, either inadvertently or on purpose. There were also reports that the eleven-hour trip from Mar del Plata to Chacarita included a stop at a private clinic, which raised more questions.

Another mystery involved the removal of the sternocleidomastoid muscle in Alicia's neck. This muscle would've shown physical evidence of her being strangled, and its removal by the first medical examiner led to suspicion of a conspiracy to protect Monzon. The only reason to remove that muscle would be to erase evidence that Alicia had been strangled. Ultimately, the removal didn't matter—Alicia's lungs showed the damage of suffocation—but for many years there was talk of skulduggery at the morgue. One of the medical experts, in a dark mood, joked that the missing piece of Alicia's neck had been fed to a cat.

There were also many people at Facha Martel's during the fatal weekend, including Martel's son, Monzon and Alicia's son, and several adults. Apparently the adults all cleared out so Monzon and Alicia could have some time alone; the two little boys remained behind, purportedly staying with the landlord on the top floor. Other guests included local realtor Daniel Comba and a twenty-year-old schoolteacher, María Alejandra Lato. It was even rumored that on the morning in question, an important theatrical entrepreneur was sleeping in Martel's garage with a well-known South American singer. Apparently, despite Alicia visiting, this was very much another typical party weekend at El Facha's. Some sources say Martel gave both Monzon and Alicia cocaine that Saturday. Was Alicia's death, some wondered, the tragic result of a coke binge? "Monzon was aggressive by nature," said Bialo. "When he added cocaine, he created an explosive cocktail."

Then there was Monzon's inability to remember details. Some wondered if this was his way of protecting others who may have been involved. "He never defended himself by telling the whole truth," Bialo said, pointing out that Monzon's initial statement had been taken without the assistance of a lawyer, that he made no mention of the people "who had been in that villa in Mar del Plata. He never spoke of those who advised him in the first moments (after the crime), nor those who participated in the fraud of the fall off the balcony."

Monzon also hurt his case by not admitting to his use of cocaine, which could've been used by his attorneys to suggest he wasn't in his right mind. "He confessed to me in the prison of Batan," said Bialo, "that he was ashamed to declare that he was drunk and drugged, since such a statement would be read by his children." According to Bialo, Monzon preferred to spend time in jail "rather than telling the country he was a drug addict."

Many believe Martel knew more about Alicia's death than he let on. Martel was at the scene that morning, retrieving his drug stash before the police arrived. It was determined that two hours passed between Alicia's fall and when the police were called. Why did it take so long? Were Monzon and Martel trying to cover up or destroy evidence? The Muniz family lawyer Rodolpho Vega Lecich noted later, "there were weapons and a quantity of drugs in the house. In that group there were people who trafficked on a large scale in Mar del Plata." Often referring to Monzon's circle of friends as "gangsters" and "mafia," Lecich depicted Monzon as nothing more than a helpful dupe. "Monzon saved them because after killing Alicia, it is believed that he threw the merchandise down the toilet."

Some speculated that Martel helped Monzon concoct his cover story during this time period. Others guessed that Martel used the time to remove the many video recordings he'd made of his sex parties because so many of his famous friends had been involved.

Martel's son Roman said in 2019 that he remembered his father waking him up as the house was swarming with police. Martel gave nine-year-old Roman a backpack filled with cocaine to be smuggled past the officers and out of the house. The police would never suspect a kid to have coke in his backpack. This was El Facha—a desperate and devious man who would stoop to using his own son this way.

Then there was the strange death of Alberto Olmedo, a famous actor who was performing in Mar del Plata that summer. A friend of Monzon and Martel who lived in the same neighborhood, Olmedo fell from a balcony and died one month after Alicia's death. Martel was suspected of giving Olmedo the cocaine that fueled his fatal drop. Martel was never charged with anything, though he was Mar del Plata's bad penny, never far away when someone fell out of a balcony.

Olmedo's estranged wife, Nancy Herrera, later described Martel as the neighborhood's "drugs and women facilitator . . . a bipolar type who sometimes felt omnipotent and thought he could fix the world in five minutes . . . he thought he was the great comedian, but he had a big ego and was always speaking badly about people." Herrera also noticed Martel acting strangely the day before Alicia's death, hiding cocaine everywhere. He'd become convinced that the police knew about his drug stash and were coming for him.

Herrera also claimed to have seen the television announcement about Monzon's arrest, which prompted her to call Olmedo. She insists that Olmedo said simply, "He choked her and threw her away." But this was days before medical examiners had announced the injuries to Alicia's throat. How did Olmedo know?

It's possible that Herrera misremembered her conversation with Olmedo.

Or had Olmedo learned something from Martel and Monzon? Had Olmedo been at the scene of the crime?

And did his knowledge have anything to do with his own mysterious death?

During the 1990s, Martel found that producers wouldn't hire him for acting jobs, though he was often invited to appear on talk shows when the discussion was about drug use in show business. He'd become the Argentine poster boy for burned-out cokehead actors. When Martel appeared on the Argentine panel show *The People Want to Know,* he endured many uncomfortable questions about Monzon and Alicia. Martel said he believed Monzon, and that Alicia's death was an accident. Shortly after this television appearance, Martel tried to commit suicide by hurling himself from an eighth-floor window. He survived. The rest of Martel's life was a mix of cocaine-related scandals, occasional acting work, and poor health. He died in 2013, with many unanswered questions about his life.

"Prosecutors never proved that a third person was in the house, and never proved Martel knew anything," said Bialo. "But Martel's personal and professional life suffered. I always felt it was wrong that so many show-business names were attached to the story, such as Olmedo. Martel was in a show, and at night he would return to his house with members of the cast, both male and female, but it seems he had agreed with Monzon to stay away on that night. The landlord swore at the trial that he hadn't seen Martel at the house during the night of the crime. Yet there were rumors of theatrical types being around the house. I believe people were mistaken."

Baez the scrap collector came under constant scrutiny. A story appeared that he'd not actually seen anything, but that a friend of his had actually witnessed the murder of Alicia. The unknown witness couldn't go to the police because he had a number of outstanding warrants. Feeling guilty, he gave the information to Baez, which explained why Baez was a few days late in going to the authorities. Another story involved Baez having once served a prison sentence for molesting his granddaughter, and that the local police sometimes pressured him into doing dirty work for them. Monzon's supporters claimed the prosecutors were so intent on busting Monzon that they forced Baez to testify against him.

It was also reported during the trial that Baez was seen in the company of a mysterious blonde woman; some wondered if this unknown female somehow goaded him into changing his testimony to make him seem less reliable. The Monzon team wasn't above sending hooligans after the judge or paying a taxi driver to give false testimony. Did they also send a femme fatale to persuade Baez?

Still, there was an even bigger bombshell involving Baez. The revelation, which sounds like a scene from an Alfred Hitchcock movie, claimed Baez had actually been inside Martel's house at the time of the murder, having broken in after hearing Alicia crying for help. He'd allegedly stood just feet away from Monzon and Alicia, before panicking and fleeing. Lecich confided to journalist Jorge Joury that Baez had burglarized many homes on Pedro Zanni Street and knew his way in and out. This fact couldn't be used in court, Lecich explained, "because they would discredit him, and say he was stealing. That's why we said he was behind a tree."

Lecich played a head game with Monzon. From the first days of the investigation, Lecich was leaking information to *Diario Popular*, which he happened to know was Monzon's favorite newspaper. Lecich wanted Monzon to be "nervous that the truth was on his heels."

But even if Monzon's favorite periodical seemed to be against him, the press wasn't always kind to Alicia. Not only did her dead body appear constantly on magazine covers, but Argentina's more chauvinistic columnists speculated that she had been unfaithful and that Monzon was merely a jealous, proud man. Typically, there were many editorials that blamed the victim. If Monzon had been so terrible, they asked, why was Alicia always coming back to him? Perhaps, they suggested, because she was using his name to help her failed modeling career.

The tone of the coverage began to change, until readers might think this wasn't a tragedy for Alicia, but a tragedy for Monzon.

◆ ◆ ◆

Meanwhile, Monzon lazed around in his cell, smoking and reading the Bible.

American actor Mickey Rourke once went to Argentina to visit him. Rourke had not only started on his own boxing career, but was supposedly going to play Monzon in a movie of his life. They met and talked and sparred a bit. According to legend, Monzon knocked Rourke unconscious with a single right hand. A spokesman for Rourke said no such thing happened, that an Argentine journalist had written a bunch of lies.

The writer was simply trying to keep the Monzon myth alive.

# Killer and Still Champion

Aside from a wacky rumor that Alain Delon was going to help Monzon break out of prison by helicopter, Monzon's years of incarceration were quiet. He didn't cause trouble. Nothing he did made news. He once signed a petition to have AIDS-infected prisoners quarantined; on another occasion he was thought to be part of a planned escape, but in actuality he had been too drunk to take part. In 1991, as Argentine junior middleweight Jorge Castro prepared to face Terry Norris for the WBC title, Monzon gave him some advice over the prison telephone. Monzon warned him not to catch cold.

There were occasional murmurs that the other cons would try to test Monzon and he would fight them off, but Monzon was actually a model prisoner, behaving himself while his contacts worked with politicians to help his cause. Gradually, Monzon was moved from Batán to prisons in Junín and then Las Flores, each a step up in comfort for Argentina's most famous convict, the latter being close to many of his friends and family in Santa Fe.

Agustin Carlos "Chiquito" Uleriche, owner of a popular Santa Fe seafood restaurant, brought Monzon lunch and dinner almost every day. "I couldn't leave him alone," said Uleriche, whose father had befriended Monzon's father years earlier. Uleriche's restaurant was wall to wall with Monzon memorabilia, and there was always an empty chair and table in Monzon's honor. Uleriche never believed Monzon was a murderer. "They fell," he said of Monzon and Alicia. "It was a tragedy."

Uleriche wasn't the only one serving Monzon. Friends brought him wine, cigarettes, and good clothes to wear. Even locked away for murder, Monzon still had his admirers under a spell. But were they merely falling for the charms of a psychopath? Monzon could get people to piss in a cup for him so he could pass a drug test. He could convince women to love him, even if had a reputation for smashing them in the face. He was a manipulator.

Behind bars, Monzon wasn't in a position to return the favors being done for him. In a way, this was his element: He was able to receive without ever having to give. Cherquis Bialo once witnessed Monzon being visited by his daughter, Sylvia, and was surprised at how little Monzon gave by way of emotional contact or acknowledgment. "There was no tender gesture from him," said Bialo. "Nothing. He didn't know how." But Monzon knew how to get what he wanted.

When a television news crew visited Monzon in Las Flores, viewers might've been surprised to see Monzon's setup. No longer in a small cell, he was now in a barracks, with several beds lined up where he and other convicts slept. At the head of his bed was a table covered with framed pictures of his children. He fumbled with a cigarette as he spoke in a quiet voice, saying that his children meant everything to him. Looking well-fed and well-dressed, he was not the broken man described in the tabloids. In 1993 he was photographed in the prison yard, drinking wine with Alain Delon, the two of them smiling like they were back on the French Riviera.

In one prison interview, Monzon announced that he was going to quit drinking forever, because drinking had caused all of his problems. In another, he said he was in prison only because of happenstance. He explained that Maxi had needed shoes, and if Monzon had gone to a shoe store with the boy and dropped him off at Alicia's, that the tragedy wouldn't have happened. As was usually the case when Monzon spoke, this contradicted everything he'd said previously about the romantic weekend he'd planned with Alicia.

Sometimes he blamed his temper. Journalist Mercedes Marti once asked Monzon what a woman might do to make him angry. "I am old-fashioned," Monzon said, adding that women should dress appropriately in public. He especially disliked when his wife showed off her legs. "Show your legs to me," he said. "I'm the husband."

Though he didn't say much about Alicia's death, Monzon once suggested she may have fallen because she was weak from diet pills. Increasingly, Monzon created a picture of himself as a simple, old-fashioned man yoked to a pill-popping, skimpily dressed, disrespectful woman.

Monzon's refusal to admit his guilt began to sound delusional. In a 1993 interview with journalist Guillermo Andino, Monzon not only denied he'd ever struck Alicia, but he blatantly rewrote history in regard to their last days together. Those days were, he said, "Very happy, we were in love. I love her, I still love her. She is still the woman of my life. I never hit her."

The man who once bragged that he hit all his women now said he'd never laid a hand on Alicia, or any female. He said his arguments with women never involved more than a few broken dinner plates. "Ask the women I had before Alicia," Monzon said.

In 1993, Monzon's good behavior resulted in a new furlough arrangement. He was allowed to spend daytime hours and weekends outside of prison. He would stay in San Javier with his son Abel on Saturday and Sunday, and during the week would serve as a boxing instructor at the UPCN (Union of Civil Personnel of the Nation) in Santa Fe. Monzon's only requirement was to return to the prison on Sunday night and weeknights. This riled Argentina's growing feminist population—and anyone else who thought a convicted murderer shouldn't be offered such freedoms.

◆ ◆ ◆

On Sunday, January 8, 1995, returning to prison after a barbecue where he presumably had been drinking, Monzon stomped the gas of the gray Renault 19 he was driving. Behind the wheel without authorization, he was clocked at approximately eighty-six miles per hour on Provincial Route One in Los Cerrillos. Observers noted he seemed to have trouble steering. Monzon lost control; the car overturned six or seven times, until it was crumpled like a sheet of tinfoil. A friend and passenger, Jerónimo Mottura, died in the wreck. Monzon's sister-in-law, Alicia Fessia, was injured but lived.

Monzon died instantly. He was fifty-two.

◆ ◆ ◆

The real Carlos Monzon can't be summed up quickly. He was not the "epic man" that Bialo dubbed him, nor was he, as Alain Delon once said, "A conquistador, and a prince." His defenders say he was merely an uneducated man who never learned how to control himself. Even the terrible end of Alicia can be bent to suit Monzon's idolaters. For them, Monzon represents the irrational, perilous side of love. When a man becomes a myth, he can be refashioned and repurposed again and again.

It was Monzon's disregard for people that drove him, and it was also his personal downfall. This sense of superiority is something many great fighters possess, and it no doubt helped Monzon get through some tough fights. For Monzon, his inflated sense of himself was a secret weapon.

But it also affected Monzon's private life. He put himself above people. His driving record illustrates his attitude. On the day he died, he was probably pushing that Renault 19 like there was no one else on the road. He wanted to be thought of as a romantic, but he loved only as far as it benefitted him. When it suited him, he would declare himself a rancher, or a simple fisherman, but he preferred the company of millionaires. At his low point, when he would've surely benefited from a simpler life, he stayed in Mar del Plata, near the action, where his name still meant something, where he'd get a good table, and a woman, and some cocaine, and reason to believe he was still the one and only Monzon.

Ultimately, his life requires more consideration than is generally given. In his mind he was always the small, vulnerable product of poverty and ignorance, so in the classic tradition of the narcissist he created a mask for himself, a kind of grandiose, all-powerful bully who was always in control. But like all narcissists, his image was fragile; he was never far from becoming completely unhinged. It is perhaps as a psychological study that Monzon is best appreciated. He was the human id unchecked.

◆ ◆ ◆

In America, raising oneself up from poverty to wealth is the underlying theme of many success stories. But in Argentina during Monzon's time, such a rise was regarded as something quasi-mystical, proof, perhaps, that God's hand reaches down from the heavens to bless a select few. Monzon, the shoeshine boy, was an ultimate example of this. "This creature," wrote Cherquis Bialo, "emerged from abject marginality, achieved fame, admiration and glory. He was received by presidents, kings and princes." Bialo and others wrote variations of this theme for decades, turning Monzon into a feel-good fable, as if Monzon had emerged from the very swamps of San Javier to mingle with the prince of Monaco. And when Monzon died in a car crash, they had the perfect tragic ending for their fable. From poverty, to glory, to prison, to tragedy. To his Argentine supporters, his sordid personal history only made him more human, a bona fide representative of the disinherited, the poor of the earth.

For countless Argentines, death absolved Monzon of his sins; the disaster on Route One was the cue to start rebuilding his image. Among the first to do so was Argentine president Carlos Menem. On the day of Monzon's funeral, as if giving the country marching orders, Menem said, "Remember Carlos Monzon as a champion, not as a man jailed for murder."

The governor of Santa Fe, Carlos Alberto Reutemann, recalled Monzon as a "disciplined, responsible man who became an idol. When Monzon fought, Argentina was paralyzed." Nino Benvenuti spoke from Rome to an Argentine news service. Remembering the fighter who took his championship, Benvenuti said, "part of my life has gone with the death of Carlos."

"He was one of the world's greatest sports figures," Benvenuti added. "He did great things and he has to be remembered for those and not for his current circumstances."

While many expounded on his greatness, Monzon's body lay in state at Santa Fe's city hall. Hundreds of floral wreaths surrounded the casket. An estimated ten thousand people, including politicians and celebrities, filed past. Another twenty thousand mourners lined the two-mile route to Santa Fe's Municipal Cemetery, chanting and tossing roses into the street. Another six thousand waited at the cemetery's entrance, flying a black-and-white banner that read, "Although a star dies, its light continues to shine. You had great humility, that's why you stay among us."

Monzon's death meant little in America. Columnists reached for comparisons to O. J. Simpson and Mike Tyson; Mickey Rourke still wanted to portray Monzon in a movie.

Some praised him as a fighter. Some didn't. Gil Clancy couldn't bring himself to say he was a fan. "Overrated," he told the *New York Daily News*. Ferdie Pacheco, who worked Napoles's corner when he faced Monzon in France, described Monzon as "unbeatable," with "perfect control of everything that was happening in that ring. People who perhaps don't understand boxing would say Monzon wasn't a good fighter because he wasn't fluid, he wasn't like a Sugar Ray Robinson or a Sugar Ray Leonard, but he was accomplishing everything that a fluid boxer could do."

Meanwhile, New York columnist Michael Katz wrote that Monzon "killed his wife by throwing her off a balcony, apparently to see how high she could bounce."

# The Outlaw Saint

In Argentina, the tributes to Monzon included the creation of two monuments, one on the Santa Fe waterfront, the second at the site of his death. Revealed to the public on October 28, 1996, the former was an enormous marble statue of Monzon, weighing a reported twenty tons and towering over tourists at a height of approximately fifty feet. It was created by Mexican sculptor Mario Rendón Lozano with some involvement from the WBC. It was oversized, garish, but strangely magnetic, much like Monzon had been. Visitors to Santa Fe still pose for pictures at the feet of the titan, usually with their fists up in a boxing stance. "For the people of Santa Fe, he isn't a murderer, " said Carlos Irusta.

The death-site statue was a depiction of Monzon in a victory pose. Though allegedly made in the exact dimensions of Monzon's body, it seemed oddly elongated, skeletal, bearing a resemblance to Giacometti's "Walking Man." It was as if the artist, Roberto Favaretto Forner, was trying with one pose to capture both the boy with rickets and the boxing champion. At night, alone on Route One, the statue must have seemed a lonely thing, haunting, the gloved hands reaching up to the stars.

On the fifteenth anniversary of Monzon's death, it was announced that the Route One statue had been vandalized; it was covered in small gashes, and a large chunk of a leg had been torn away. A citizen "watch-dog" unit formed in 2014 to protect Forner's sculpture, but vandals still bashed away at it, while demonstrators against gender abuse protested its existence. A killer of a woman, they argued, shouldn't be honored in a public space. Someone spray-painted the monument's base with "Where there is violence there is no love."

Forner went about restoring the statue in 2015, having it hauled back to his studio for repairs. There were fundraising events to help with expenses, and a massive donation of materials, including keys, bits of plumbing, anything that could be melted down and used. Even Monzon's family got involved in the effort to repair the piece. At a press conference, Monzon's daughter, Sylvia, chastised those who would disrespect an idol, and reminded people that her father was the country's greatest fighter, the man who made the rest of the world notice Argentina.

While Forner's statue was back in the workshop, women's groups began picketing the Santa Fe memorial. Inspired by Mexican artist Elina Chauvet's Red Shoes Project—her installations involve hundreds of red shoes placed in public squares to draw awareness to violence against women—Argentine demonstrators began leaving red shoes at the base of the waterfront statue. In 2018, a political group created a mock plaque and affixed it to the monument. It read, "Carlos Monzon, Campeon Mundial y Femicida." ("Carlos Monzon, World Champion and Woman Killer.")

The plaque was a pointed reference to a phenomenon in Argentina, namely, that tributes to Monzon increasingly ignored Alicia's murder altogether, as if Monzon's personal life was best left out of the story.

To the surprise of Monzon's admirers, Forner announced on Facebook in 2019 that he wouldn't be returning his statue to the Route One location. He agreed with the women's groups that Monzon shouldn't be honored; the sculpture would remain in his workshop. Since his announcement, the statue has only been seen in photographs appearing on Santa Fe news sites. It was on its back, on a dolly. Surrounded by Forner's other works and half-finished projects, it seems pitiable, unrealized. If it looks like anything, it resembles an old-time fairground mummy, the sort carnival hustlers used to foist on a gullible public, something like P. T. Barnum's mermaid or the Cardiff Giant. It's neither dangerous nor inspiring. It's not even a signal to drivers to slow down so you don't end up like Monzon.

The massive monument on Santa Fe's waterfront appears unmovable. Despite protests from women's groups, it remains in place, high and imposing. An online tourist site called WelcomeArgentina.com mentions the statue as a favorite destination of visitors to the area, describing Monzon as having earned "the love of all Argentinian people." The online brochure makes no mention of his conviction for murder, only that Monzon was "not such a lucky man outside the ring."

Curiously, the description adds, "Nobody can judge him."

◆ ◆ ◆

Alicia Muniz's death has been credited with an increased awareness of spousal abuse in Argentina and the introduction of the term "femicide" into Argentine murder trials. Ironically, when the anniversary of Alicia's death is recalled, it now falls on a holiday that Argentina didn't recognize in 1988: Valentine's Day.

The Monzon case also brought awareness to the growing cocaine problem in Mar del Plata. The fact that Alicia's family paid their legal fees with help from local church officials—Lecich's firm promptly donated their fee to a children's hospital—is viewed by some as an early round in Argentina's ongoing battle between the Church and drug traffickers. Mar del Plata has almost returned to its one-time glory as a shining seaside resort. Drugs and crime still exist there, but the La Florida neighborhood is not quite the crime-riddled enclave it used to be. Many feel Mar del Plata never recovered from the deaths of Alicia Muniz and Alberto Olmedo. Journalist Camilo Sanchez has written extensively on the subject and believes that the city reached a kind of golden age and then, with the two tragedies, withered. "It was like the full moon; at some point it begins to wane."

Tito Lectoure bought the house on Pedro Zanni Street and kept it in his family for many years. For much of that time, the place was a destination for ghoulish sightseers wanting to see the exact spot where Alicia Muniz landed. Some people even brought mattresses for overnight stays, hoping to sleep on the very bricks where Alicia died. These days the community is heavily gated. The official word is that the gates were put up to prevent burglaries, but it was mostly to discourage morbid tourists.

◆ ◆ ◆

It snuck on to Argentine television sets in June of 2019, a thirteen-part miniseries called *Monzon.* Airing on Space, a Latin American pay channel owned by Warner Media, the purported biography of Monzon was riddled with inaccuracies, the most glaring being a fictional subplot that linked Monzon to a major drug-trafficking ring. Spread out over the entire Argentine winter, viewers had to wait for the concluding episode to see the program's interpretation of what happened back in February of 1988. "You're a whore!" yells Jorge Ramon, the actor playing Monzon, as he throttles Carla Quevedo as Alicia. Once he realizes she's dead, he releases a wail of grief. In the series finale, Monzon killed Alicia out of jealousy. Twenty-four years after his death, Monzon had been reborn as Othello.

A stylish but dull police procedural, *Monzon* was a ratings success in Argentina. It features lots of dour investigators, forensic experts, nosy reporters, re-creations of old news broadcasts, and, of course, Monzon, usually in very tight underwear or brooding in a cell. This isn't a Monzon who hits women; he tends to yell and pound on tables. Executive producers Pol and Agustin Bossi, who had helmed everything from comedies to horror movies, evoked Monzon as his fellow Argentines must wish to remember him. As the prison-bound Monzon of 1988, Roman is all scowls; the young

Monzon, played by Mauricio Paniagua, is doe-eyed, sensitive, a shirtless romantic, a good father to his children. Monzon is depicted as something of a martyr, a notion encouraged by an opening credit montage that blends clips of his fights with a shot of Jesus on the cross.

The linking of Monzon to Jesus sounds absurd but fits in with Argentina's penchant for "outlaw saints," where the poor have historically worshipped less than saintly figures; when a popular Argentine singer known as Gilda died in a bus crash in 1996, her fans began referring to her as "Saint Gilda" and attributed miracles to her. Many Argentine folk legends involve a painful demise and, if not a Christ-like resurrection, at least a presence reaching out from the afterlife. With his own horrible highway death, Monzon may be on the way to his own kind of outlaw sainthood.

As expected, the series brought out many of Monzon's supporters. One of his lawyers, Patricia Perelló, appeared on television to declare that Monzon "never received a fair trial." Actress Graciela Borges, who once worked with Monzon, said in 2019, "I'm sure he never wanted to kill Alicia. Do you know why? Because he loved her with all his soul." She added, "But when he drank, alcohol transformed him." Monzon's daughter, Sylvia, said Alicia's death was an accident that "could've happened to anyone." She also alleged that her father didn't hit women unless they provoked him, a notion that didn't sit well with modern feminists. Her brother Abel dismissed the series as "sensationalism."

The veteran sportswriters who had covered Monzon's career also cashed in, rehashing old stories for Argentine websites. Bialo, always Monzon's top rooter, called the program's depiction of Monzon "a rude caricature," adding that the show skipped over his greatness as a fighter.

Meanwhile, a seventy-year-old former model, Vicky Antille, came forth to declare she had been Monzon's secret wife throughout the 1970s. Author Maria Laura Silvera announced she was collaborating on a book with a woman who allegedly fell in love with Monzon while he was in prison.

These voices from the past were an odd juxtaposition next to the younger journalists who railed at the authorities for not putting Monzon away for life. The old guard remained protective of Monzon, still depicting him as an unfortunate fellow who couldn't handle the pressures of fame. In a way, it was the season of Monzon, his stormy life unveiled like an old WPA mural, cracked and chipped with age, but still colorful, still stirring.

No one benefited from the wave of Monzon nostalgia more than Susana Gimenez.

Since her days with Carlos, she'd become the highest-paid television personality in Argentina, a status achieved by endorsing beauty products and hosting her popular self-titled talk show. Well into her seventies, she took advantage of *Monzon* by inviting several members of the cast, as well as Monzon's family members, onto her program. In 2005 she'd invited Monzon's first wife, Mercedes, to be on her program; the two women cried in each other's arms. Here was another opportunity to exploit her most notorious relationship. Susana smartly parceled the appearances out to last the entire run of the show. The atmosphere was strangely jovial, even celebratory. She complimented the actors on the great job they'd done, though she insisted Monzon wasn't as bad as portrayed in the series.

Monzon's grandson Augustin appeared on an episode with Susana. An eighteen-year-old who looked like a softer version of his granddad, Augustin asked many coy questions about Monzon's relationship with Susana. At times, the young man seemed to be flirting with his grandfather's former girlfriend. "You're very much like Carlos," Susana said. There was laughter all around.

Watching it, you wondered if someone in the audience would stand and shout, *Carlos Monzon was a son of a bitch—a murderer*!

But nothing happened. Week after week, for the entire summer, Susana's show was nothing but smiles and laughter. Everyone had a wonderful time.

Why bring up a little thing like murder?

◆ ◆ ◆

Rather poignantly, the only child of Monzon and Alicia, now near forty, came out of the shadows to speak during the release of the Space series. Maximiliano doesn't appear in public often. His life has been difficult, with many stints in therapy and drug rehab facilities. He has been contacted for interviews in the past but would only speak under strict conditions, such as no questions about his parents, and that he only be interviewed by mail, not in person. His therapists at the Gradiva clinic in Buenos Aires once described him as having "the character of a disabled person," and thus he required judicial protection from the press.

Without easy access to him, tabloid journalists have made a hobby of Max, printing stories that he was not only a drug addict but was also, among other things, a transvestite. They have followed him with cameras, harassed him, and have no doubt driven him into reclusiveness. He is wary of the public, especially on the anniversary of his mother's death. "Many find out who you are," he said, "and seek to do something to you." He solved some of his fears by moving to Santa Fe, where his father's memory is still dear. But as those in drug recovery often say, Max finds life to be "an everyday struggle. I can't trust myself, because drugs and substances are everywhere."

Max is fascinated by his father's legacy as a fighter, which still echoes across the landscape. Of average size and build, with his father's strong features and the wide-set eyes of his mother, he emerged from the rubble of his family with a unique set of anxieties. He has gradually accepted his peculiar life, one where he lost his mother at age six and his father at thirteen. Despite everything, Max feels his father still deserves admiration, if only for overcoming such poverty. "That's why I say his life was full of nuances. He had only a second-grade education, and suddenly achieved so much."

Max served as a consultant on the television series, and like many members of his extended family, he found himself in the public eye during the show's run in Argentina. In a rare interview, he told *Diario El Litoral* that his father made "mistakes," but deserved to be treated fairly. As for Monzon's behavior outside of boxing, Max sounded like a typical sycophant. "You have to separate things," he said, "because my father was required to behave as if he had studied at Harvard, and we know that it was not so."

Like so many of his father's admirers, Max pays less attention to the murder of Alicia ("I know it didn't happen . . .") and focuses on Monzon, the great champion. "I know that if my old man were alive, we would have a good relationship because he loved me very much and talked to me. But I also keep my distance from his 'image,' because the image wasn't anything."

Yet the image prevails. The macho man of the ring and the movies, whose marble effigy still dwarfs tourists on the Santa Fe waterfront, endures. But Monzon's real legacy may be the ongoing tension between those who idolize him and those who wish to forget him. "Appreciation for a person goes beyond certain things," said Carlos Irusta. "Maybe I'm saying something politically incorrect. A friendly journalist, who has passed away, confessed to me: 'Monzon is no longer my friend because he killed the woman.' It's understandable. I had a hard time. Deep down, I begged God that (the murder) was not real. It was."

Cherquis Bialo, perhaps the journalist who was closest to Monzon, has rarely described him as a murderer. He will say "Alicia fell" or "both had been drinking," but his conversation never veers into broken hyoid bones. For Bialo, Monzon is a near-mythical figure, an Argentine Icarus who flew too close to the sun, or in Monzon's case, the spotlight, and came hurtling back to earth. He'll describe Monzon as irrational, or dangerous, but never a murdering psychopath.

"There is a part of Monzon's life that is difficult to explain," Bialo said in 2019. "He never showed tenderness. It was hard for him to say, 'I love you.' It was easy for him to be aggressive, but I never saw him cry, or show great happiness, not with his children, not with his famous friends, not even after his greatest triumphs. He moved from one place to another, but he remained the same needy, deprived creature, no different from when he'd been born. When I search for a way to treat his memory, the only answer that satisfies me is 'mercy.'"

Still, Max feels Monzon wouldn't have asked for mercy. His mission was to be a great boxing champion, and he succeeded. "He was a born winner," Max said. The debate about him doesn't even matter. "I know that there are many women who were victims of violence. But my old man is dead. I understand that it is a sensitive issue, but I repeat, he's already dead."

The gargantuan but tarnished figure that is the Monzon of today still can't overshadow the natural wonder that he was in the 1970s. Other fighters won titles, Monzon ruled his weight class as if he were a Viking lord; he gave his countrymen a source of pride, and added a dash of glamour to what is basically a slum sport. It's reasonable why his detractors wish to punish him beyond the grave: he was an abuser of women, and he was convicted of murdering Alicia Muniz. But demonizing Carlos Monzon has yet to completely diminish his heroic side. It's as if people are still throwing trash at him, and he only grows stronger. The battle between a man's professional achievements and his personal life, champion and murderer, macho men and feminists, goes on with no sign of ending. He's proof that these arguments are eternal, and that some of us are so badly in need of an idol that we'll even praise a killer.

◆ ◆ ◆

He'd spent the last hours of his life on a riverbank. He'd been invited to a barbecue in the small town of Cayasta, fifty miles from Santa Fe. He enjoyed some roast piglet and even took a dip in the San Javier River, the same river he'd played in as a boy. A photograph was taken of him. Despite looking somewhat bloated, Monzon looks approximately the way we'd expect him to look as a fifty-two-year-old man.

By the rules of his furlough agreement, he had to be back at the Las Flores prison by 8 p.m. He didn't want to risk being late. He only had a short time left to serve on his sentence and didn't want any infractions on his record. So he drove fast. He'd always been a terrible driver. Being in prison hadn't made him any better at it.

Monzon didn't wear his seat belt. It was too warm for such things, the temperature that day having soared well over ninety degrees. As he drove, he wanted to hear the radio transmission of the day's soccer match. Monzon was passionate about Club Atlético Colón, and especially loved the commentary of Ricardo Porta, one of the few journalists he'd ever liked. Porta was one of the very few who had given him a chance against Benvenuti all those years ago. Monzon asked his sister-in-law, Alicia Fessia, to find the game on the radio. She fumbled with the dial but Porta's familiar voice wouldn't come in.

"Let me," Monzon said. With no belt restraining him, he could lean over and search the radio dial for LT9 from Santa Fe.

As he searched, he lost control of the Renault.

According to Fessia, the only survivor of the crash, Monzon died trying to find a soccer match on the radio.

Fessia climbed out of the car as a local man appeared on the scene. "Please help him!" she said. "Help save Carlos Monzon!"

She didn't know Monzon was already dead.

She also didn't know there was no soccer that day. The league was on a break.

Monzon's body was pulled from the wreckage and laid down in some high weeds. Fessia continued screaming for help as one person, then another, arrived to see what was going on. A few pictures of Monzon's corpse appeared in Argentine magazines. By the time the photos were taken, his eyes had been closed. It was said that before the photographers got there, Monzon's eyes had been wide open. He had the appearance of a man on his back, staring up at the sky. With one shoe on, and one shoe off, his hair matted by the day's swim, his belly and face somewhat swollen from years of drinking, he could've been some homeless man, one who had wandered for too long in the heat, lost his way, and decided it was time for a much-needed rest.

## SELECTED SOURCES

The following Spanish-language publications and websites were useful in the writing of this book: airedigital.com, bigbangnews.com, canchallena.com, *Caras*, *Clarin*, *Contexto*, detapasjorgejoury.blogspot.com, *El Litoral*, *El Mundo*, enganche.com, infobae.com, *La Capital de Mar del Plata*, *La Nacion*, *La Semana*, *Latinta*, MundoD.com, ole.com, and wander-argentina.com.

American sources include the Associated Press, the United Press, the *New York Daily News*, the *New York Sun*, the *New York Times*, the *Philadelphia Daily News*, the *Los Angeles Times*, the *Washington Post*, plus such publications as *The Ring*, *Boxing Illustrated*, *Sports Illustrated*, *Ringside Seat*, and *Psychology Today*.

## SPECIAL THANKS

A very special thanks to the following people for sharing their memories and insights: Nigel Collins, J Russell Peltz, Carlos Irusta, and especially Ernesto Cherquis Bialo.

Carlos Monzon published two ghostwritten memoirs in his lifetime, one in Argentina and one in France. They are very hard to find, but snippets of them appear on infobae.com.

## ABOUT THE AUTHOR

Don Stradley is an award-winning writer whose work has appeared in various publications, including *The Ring, Ringside Seat*, and ESPN.com. Along with his boxing coverage, he is the author of two previous books in the Hamilcar Noir series, *Berserk: The Shocking Life and Death of Edwin Valero* and *Slaughter in the Streets: When Boston Became Boxing's Murder Capital*. When not writing about sports, he's written about the movies for such magazines as *Cinema Retro* and *Noir City*.

*A Fistful of Murder* is set in 9.5-point Palatino, which was designed by Hermann Zapf and released initially in 1949 by the Stempel foundry and later by other companies, most notably the Mergenthaler Linotype Company. Named after the sixteenth-century Italian master of calligraphy Giovanni Battista Palatino, Palatino is based on the humanist typefaces of the Italian Renaissance, and reflects Zapf's expertise as a calligrapher. Copyeditor for this project was Shannon LeMay-Finn. The book was designed by Brad Norr Design, Minneapolis, Minnesota, and typeset by New Best-set Typesetters Ltd. Printed and manufactured by Sheridan Books using acid-free paper.

## ALSO READ

**HAMILCAR NOIR** | TRUE CRIME LIBRARY **#1**

**"There's no telling what went on during the next few hours, or where his paranoia took him, but in that room something terrible happened. At 5:30 a.m. Valero appeared in the lobby. As calmly as one might order something from room service, he told the staff that he had just killed his wife."**

Edwin Valero's life was like a rocket shot into a wall. With a perfect knockout record in twenty-seven fights, the demonic Venezuelan seemed destined for a clash with all-time-great Manny Pacquiao. But the Fates had other ideas.

Don Stradley captures one of the darkest and most sensational boxing stories in recent memory, which, until now, has never been fully told. Filled with firsthand accounts from the men who trained Valero and the reporters who covered him, as well as insights from psychologists and forensic experts, *Berserk* is a hell-ride of a book.

**Find *Berserk* at your favorite bookstore or online retailer! Or order online at www.hamilcarpubs.com.**

ISBN 9781949590142 | Paperback | November 2019

HAMILCAR NOIR

HARD-HITTING TRUE CRIME

## ALSO READ

**HAMILCAR NOIR** | TRUE CRIME LIBRARY **#2**

**"I f I wake up, I know I'm a success. The day I don't wake up, I know I'll be home. I have one foot on this earth and one foot has crossed over. I didn't just die, I lived."**
**—Johnny Tapia**

**The ghost of Johnny Tapia lives on.**

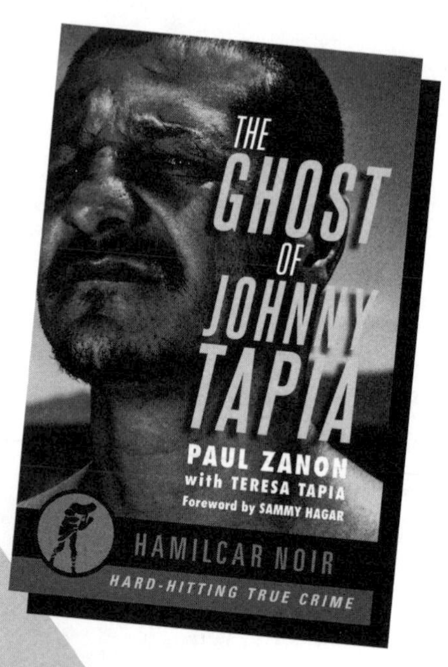


*Mi Vida Loca* ("My Crazy Life") was Johnny Tapia's nickname and his reason for being. Haunted by the brutal murder of his beloved mother when he was a child, he craved escape through boxing and drugs—and he did both with gusto.

In *The Ghost of Johnny Tapia*, Paul Zanon, with the help of Tapia's widow, Teresa, tells the harrowing and unforgettable story of a boxing genius who couldn't, in the end, defeat his demons.

**Find *The Ghost of Johnny Tapia* at your favorite bookstore or online retailer! Or order online at www.hamilcarpubs.com.**

ISBN 9781949590159 | Paperback | November 2019

HAMILCAR NOIR

*HARD-HITTING TRUE CRIME*

## ALSO READ

**HAMILCAR NOIR** | TRUE CRIME LIBRARY **#3**

**"A female stenographer who had been at her desk filling out Christmas cards looked on in horror; the sound of guns a moment earlier had shattered the holiday mood, and now she was confronted by the sight of Frankie in the doorway, blood gushing from his wounds. Without saying a word, he walked in and sat in a chair. Then he pitched forward, dead."**

Boston was once a thriving boxing city. And it was also host to an ever-expanding underworld. From the early days of Boston's Mafia, to the era of Whitey Bulger, many of the city's boxers found themselves drawn to the criminal life. Most of them ended up dead. *Slaughter in the Streets*, by Don Stradley, tells the violent and often tragic story of these misguided young men who thought their toughness in the ring could protect them from the most cold-blooded killers in the country.

**Find *Slaughter in the Streets* at your favorite bookstore or online retailer! Or order online at www.hamilcarpubs.com.**

ISBN 9781949590258 | Paperback | February 2020

HAMILCAR NOIR

HARD-HITTING TRUE CRIME

## ALSO READ

**HAMILCAR NOIR** | TRUE CRIME LIBRARY **#4**

**A new husband and father, Arturo "Thunder" Gatti seemed ready to leave the business of blood behind. Two years later, however, he was found dead in a hotel in Brazil under mysterious circumstances. He was only thirty-seven.**

Arturo Gatti was due a long, happy retirement. "Thunder" hung up his gloves in 2007, closing the book on a career that bordered on the mythical. His retirement was celebrated—boxing's modern gladiator had earned his freedom. Then he was dead.

In *Killed in Brazil?: The Mysterious Death of Arturo "Thunder" Gatti*, Jimmy Tobin uncovers the sensational events surrounding the demise of one of the most beloved fighters of recent memory.

**Find *Killed in Brazil?* at your favorite bookstore or online retailer! Or order online at www.hamilcarpubs.com.**

ISBN 9781949590265 | Paperback | April 2020

HAMILCAR NOIR

***HARD-HITTING TRUE CRIME***